Darling Ro and the Benét Women

Darling Ro

and the

Benét Women

Evelyn Helmick Hively

THE KENT STATE UNIVERSITY PRESS
Kent, Ohio

Frontispiece: Rosemary Carr Benét. Courtesy of Thomas Carr Benét.

© 2011 by The Kent State University Press, Kent, Ohio 44242

Permission to use the following material is gratefully acknowledged: letters and journals of Rosemary and Stephen Vincent Benét, used by permission of Thomas Carr Benét and the Yale Collection of American Literature, Beinecke Rare Book and Manuscript Library; letters of Elinor Wylie, used by permission of the Yale Collection of American Literature, Beinecke Rare Book and Manuscript Library; passages from "Our Paris Letter," used by permission of *Town and Country;* "Pussycat, Pussycat, Where Have You Been?" as seen in U.S. *Harper's Bazaar,* used by permission of the Hearst Corporation; "Twinkle, Twinkle, Little Star," © 1931 Condé Nast, all rights reserved, originally published in *Vogue.* Reprinted by permission.

Library of Congress Catalog Card Number 2011000685
ISBN 978-1-60635-096-6
Manufactured in the United States of America

LIBRARY OF CONGRESS CATALOGING-IN-PUBLICATION DATA
Hively, Evelyn Helmick.
Darling Ro and the Benét women / Evelyn Helmick Hively.
    p.   cm.
Includes bibliographical references and index.
ISBN 978-1-60635-096-6 (hardcover : alk. paper) ∞
1. Benét, Rosemary, 1900–1962. 2. Authors, American—20th century—Biography.
3. Benét, Rosemary, 1900–1962—Correspondence. 4. Benét, Rosemary,
1900–1962—Marriage. 5. Benét, Stephen Vincent, 1898–1943—Marriage. I. Title.
  PS3503.E53Z69 2011
  811'.52—dc22
                                2011000685

British Library Cataloging-in-Publication data are available.

15 14 13 12 11   5 4 3 2 1

For Thomas Carr Benét

The keeper of the flame

Sleep in the dust beside me, you
Who never said a faithless word
Or gave a kiss that was not true
No matter how the dust was stirred.

—Stephen Vincent Benét

Contents

Preface

Rosemary Carr Benét came to my attention as I researched material for a study of Elinor Wylie. I found much interesting information in an exhibition of the letters of the women of the Benét family at the Beinecke Rare Book and Manuscript Library at Yale University; in addition to the Wylie correspondence, there were remarkable letters written by Rosemary. The notes I began to take then had to wait for several years while I published two books on Wylie. By that time, Rosemary's son, Thomas Carr Benét, had donated many new letters and documents, which are the basis for this portrait.

For nearly ten years now I have known of Rosemary, my admiration increasing as I learn more. Everyone who wrote about her describes her charm. Frances Rose Benét, her mother-in-law, and Elinor Wylie, her sister-in-law, both called her "Darling Ro." But she is interesting for reasons beyond her lovableness: she was a talented writer; she was the muse and collaborator of an important poet; and although she was not labeled a feminist, her attitudes were those of the new independent women of the twenties. But no woman, however strong and talented, is an island. Rosemary's entire story emerges only as she interacts with an extraordinarily fascinating collection of family and friends and an ever-larger world. It is in those relationships that her strength is most apparent.

This is a chronicle of Rosemary's interests and concerns during the decade of the 1920s, focusing on the Stephen Benéts' life in Paris. Dividing history into decades for study often seems artificial, but in this case, the twenties form a distinctive entity with a beginning, middle, and end. The first stage of the Benét marriage mirrored that arc. These years for them were the shining moments of youth and love when they met people who would be lifelong friends and developed the talents that contributed much to American literature. These also were years in which Rosemary and Rachel Carr, her physician mother living in Chicago, corresponded frequently, revealing much about their families, their friends, and the era.

The couple's young friends would become some of the most interesting artists of the twentieth century. They were in Paris to study, to feed off one other's energy, and to enjoy life's pleasures on meager incomes. They formed a small American community far different from that of the famous expatriates like Hemingway and Fitzgerald, who chose France because of a sense of alienation from the political and social life in the States. For all of them, what they found in Paris in the twenties helped to influence the direction of twentieth-century culture.

Rosemary's friends included artists worthy of having their own stories told, and many have had biographies written about them. Here, they are secondary characters, brought into the narrative only as their lives intersect with Rosemary's. Even her famous husband appears only as she writes about him or as an explanation for her concerns. He, above all, deserves a new biography, in light of his role not only as a great epic poet but as a political writer who helped formulate the United States' policies of the thirties and forties.

There is little information about Rosemary's life in the twenties available beyond her letters. Charles Fenton's biography of Stephen Benét almost ignores her, and a single essay on their relationship in a collection by Izzo and Konkle was written before Thomas Benét's recent donation of Rosemary's correspondence. Most of the letters that I quote are uncataloged, and precise citations are often impossible. The letters, frequently not dated, are not necessarily in chronological order in the library folders. In some instances a reader has added dates, a few of which are clearly wrong. For these reasons I have not cluttered the endnotes with citations that give little or no information beyond that in the text. For letters without citations, I have tried to give as much information in the chronological narrative as necessary for locating the sources in the Benét materials at the Beinecke Library. For letters found in other collections at the Beinecke or elsewhere, full citations are in the endnotes.

Acknowledgments

Many people have helped me to discover the events of Rosemary Carr Benét's life in Paris and New York in the 1920s. Her son, Thomas Carr Benét, tirelessly answered questions and provided letters and photographs; the story can be told because of his recent donation of material to the Yale Collection of American Literature in the Beinecke Rare Book and Manuscript Library. His nieces, Melanie Mahin and Rosemary Birkholz, sent photographs from their private collections.

The Beinecke Library provided the superb assistance that I have found there since my graduate research in the 1960s. Patricia Willis, curator of American literature, again offered advice and encouragement for the project. Steve Young and his many assistants were knowledgeable and helpful in my navigating through material not yet cataloged.

The vice president of Books of Discovery, Melinda Blair Helmick, read an early version of the manuscript and offered many valuable suggestions, and Nancy Potter sent interesting information about the background and people of the twenties. Linda Nardi of *Town and Country,* Leigh Montville of *Vogue,* and Lisa Luna of *Harper's Bazaar* helped to negotiate the inclusion of Rosemary's early writing in the book.

For the third time, the staff at the Kent State University Press made the long process of publishing a joy. I thank Joyce Harrison, Mary Young, Susan Cash, and Will Underwood for their professional guidance and good-humored communications. To my first editor at the Press, Joanna Hildebrand Craig, I owe more than I can say.

As ever, I am grateful for the constant support of three wonderful people, Jon Sommer Helmick, Jennifer Thomas Helmick, and Melinda Blair Helmick.

CHAPTER 1

Introductions

This was meant to be just Rosemary Benét's story. As it begins she was in her twenties, her most glamorous years. The twentieth century was likewise in its twenties, one of the most exciting in memory. And Paris was full of talented young Americans—writers, artists, and musicians who came to embrace the pleasures of that world as they studied and worked. Rosemary was ready to be part of the scene: she was bright, beautiful, and talented enough to move quickly from her college graduation to a position in Paris with the international edition of the *Herald Tribune*.

Her story remained for a time a kind of fairy tale of expectations, accomplishments, and love, especially after she met the poet Stephen Vincent Benét. Soon, however, it included additional characters capable of directing the events in her life, sometimes as positive influences in her rise to achievement and prominence. A few, however, demonstrated the truth of Sartre's declaration about Hell and other people. Some were a mixture of both. But they were often people whose personalities and talents made them powerful in their influence over others, the young Rosemary among them.

Brief introductions are necessary for the fascinating men and women who make up the secondary dramatis personae of the account of Rosemary's love affair with Stephen Vincent Benét and Paris in the 1920s. Primary among them are her parents. At home in Illinois, she had been the well-loved child of successful professionals. Thomas Carr, an exceptionally handsome naval officer, served as a deputy in the new Chicago branch of the naval office and, when that office closed, later worked as deputy collector and inspector in the Treasury Department. He had been prominent enough in Washington, D.C., circles that newspapers reported his visit as guest of Senator and Mrs. Stubblefield. Chicago papers mentioned his trips to Ireland, England, and France to buy horses in his capacity as a member of the Percheron Society and praised his efforts to help a soldier appeal a sentence.

Rosemary's mother, Dr. Rachel Hickey Carr, one of the first women physicians to practice in Chicago, served as president of the Medical Women's Association. In 1889 she was one of three women doctors who, in spite of government commands to stay away, left their practices to serve the victims of the Johnstown Flood. Dr. Carr was modern in many ways, especially in her knowledge of nutrition, which she used to full advantage in her supervision of Rosemary's diet, wherever she was. But she was truly old-fashioned in treating patients as guests in her home, often examining them on her own bed. She reasoned that patients did not like the paraphernalia of doctors' offices. While maintaining her practice, she also served as medical director for the Peoples Life Insurance Company of Illinois. Few women could boast of the kind of evaluation that her son-in-law, Stephen Vincent Benét, wrote to Laura, his sister: "She's a wonderful person and there's nobody like her. And of course her life story is really an epic—particularly her early years—I always listen with fascination."[1]

In another remarkable physician Rosemary found a second influential maternal figure. The doctor at her delivery was Rachel's friend Bertha Van Hoosen, who taught at Northwestern University, the University of Illinois, and Loyola. Before Rosemary was born, Rachel Carr had miscarried twice, and Dr. Van Hoosen's strong feelings of responsibility for this child made her become a part of the family, even taking Rosemary to her farm during the summer. Her many medical innovations included the world's smallest appendix incision, the first mother's milk bureau in the United States (she sent a supply to the famous Canadian Dionne quintuplets), her advocacy of sex education, and her use of the "twilight zone" for women in childbirth. Her memoir, *Petticoat Surgeon*, is a vivid account of an extraordinary life. In 1940, at age seventy-seven, she was still operating four days a week.[2] After growing up among such vital people, especially these two women, Rosemary felt their influence always.

The Benéts, too, were an extraordinarily close family, even though they lived across the ocean from each other during most of the twenties. Stephen's father, James Walker Benét, was from a distinguished family of Spanish descent that settled in St. Augustine in 1785. Like his father, Brigadier General Stephen Vincent Benét, Colonel Benét was a West Point graduate. At home he was a strong taskmaster, a patriot, a moralist, and a lover of literature. According to a poet friend, "He knew more about English poetry than most poets and all professors."[3]

Frances Neill Rose, Stephen's mother, was from Carlisle, Pennsylvania, where her great-grandfather on the Neill side of the family had been president of Dickinson College. Described as "charming and highly cultivated," she thought of herself as a poet but devoted her strength and talent to running her family. The relationship between the strong-willed parents was not always smooth, and during some periods the young Stephen was left behind at the army base with his father while his mother stayed in Carlisle. At one point when Mrs. Benét considered leaving, she wrote to her elder son, William, at Yale, "Your Father has no real love for children. He enjoys Tib's [Stephen's] funny remarks, but not his companionship—never makes any arrangement for them to be together."[4] She added that it was a great pity. Yet Stephen's mature poetry owed much to his early education at home, where he absorbed much information from his military milieu, as well as habits of discipline and devotion to his country. He always maintained that his father was his most important influence in every way.

The Benét family included William Rose, Stephen's older brother, who was a poet, novelist, and critic widely admired and respected both for his literary talents and for his generous help to young writers. With Henry Canby, William established the *Saturday Review* in 1924. His first wife, Teresa Thompson, died in the 1919 influenza epidemic, leaving him with three young children. Teresa's sister, Kathleen Norris, was called "America's most beloved novelist" during the twenties. She was at the same time loved and admired by the Benét family, especially Rosemary. She and her husband, Charles Gilman Norris, also a writer, took William's three children to live at their beautiful ranch in California until they were adults.

William's second marriage, to Elinor Wylie, a critically acclaimed poet and novelist who was as well known for her beauty and tempestuous life as for her literary talent, kept alive controversy and emotional outbursts that often had an impact on the lives of Rosemary and Stephen. The scandals surrounding Elinor's politically and socially prominent family were frequent fodder for the New York and Washington newspapers and a source of embarrassment for Colonel and Mrs. Benét.

All the members of the family seemed destined to pursue literary careers. Laura, the oldest of the three Benét siblings, worked in various editorial positions, living with her parents during her youth when her health was fragile. She maintained close friendships with the poets Marianne Moore and Lola Ridge. Later in her life she wrote much poetry and several biographies.

The colonel's brother, Laurence Benét, was one of the most powerful Americans in France in the twenties as a director of the Societé Hotchkiss et Compagnie, an armaments manufacturer. He ruled the American colony in Paris, along with his wife, the imperious Margaret Cox Benét. An American newspaper, writing on Paris events, reported frequently on Mrs. Benét, "whose word is law in several smart circles in that city." Aunt Margaret was of great help in introducing the young Stephen to the upper reaches of Parisian society, but at the same time she caused small commotions by trying to exert her control over the entire family. She was a figure of both deference and slight ridicule to the younger Americans in Paris.

In addition to her family, those who were most important in Rosemary's life in these early years in France were often the men who had been Stephen's classmates and their wives. The friendships formed at Yale were exceptionally strong during the war years, and they continued and strengthened whenever they were together in Paris or New York. A number of them quickly became notables in the world of the arts.

One remarkable friend was John Chipman Farrar, editor of the *Yale Literary Magazine* and, in the 1920s, the *Bookman*, a leading journal in New York, and later a founder of successful publishing houses. He remained close to Stephen, who called him his "log-roller," referring to Farrar's help at Yale and in the promotion of Benét's later poetry. Another literary classmate was Philip Barry, a writer of works for theater, television, and movies, whose early success made him one of the wealthiest of the Benét circle. He and his wife, Ellen, lavishly entertained their Yale friends both at their villa in France and in New York.

Douglas Moore, composer, conductor, and educator, was already studying in Paris when Stephen and Rosemary arrived. He had been two classes ahead of Stephen at Yale and remembered the excitement of the members of the literary Elizabethan Club on the arrival of the published poet in 1915. Moore was a major figure in American music of the twentieth century.

The Moores introduced Rosemary and Stephen to other interesting Americans in Paris. One couple, Richard and Alice Lee Myers, helped to maintain the unity of the "gang" for decades. Myers was a bon vivant and a talented composer but made his living in France as a manager with the American Express Company and later as an editor of the *Ladies' Home Journal.* Both he and Alice Lee had graduated from the University of Chicago, where she had been a member of Rosemary's sorority, the Esoterics, a few years before Rosemary. She worked in the fashion industry and wrote a fashion column from Paris for the *Chicago Daily News.* Rosemary referred to her as "our pocket guide to etiquette."

Once the Benéts began work in the United States, one of the most important figures in their professional lives was Carl Brandt, perhaps the most influential literary agent of the twenties. As one writer said of him, he not only took care of his clients' financial interests but also gave constant and intelligent criticism. He once called Stephen "the finest person I ever knew" and wrote to Rosemary at the time of Stephen's death, "It is true, possibly, that my reason for being is that I could, in small ways, be of use to him. He has given me the chance, in my time, to know the freedoms which were his absolutes. All I can hope for is to live up to his vision."[5] The meeting of Stephen Vincent Benét and Carl Brandt was the beginning of an alliance, both personal and professional, of two talented men of integrity who contributed much to the literary world of the twentieth century.

Closest to Rosemary, both in Paris and in New York until a tragic death in 1925, was Catharine Hopkins, an artist who created popular paper dolls in several magazines and did charming illustrations for *Vogue.* Catharine's many casual love affairs were the subject of gentle teasing from her close friends, but the matter of her torturous alliance with Condé Nast, the publisher of *Vanity Fair* and *House and Garden,* was of concern to all.

This remarkable group of strong, talented, and often demanding people created Rosemary and Stephen's social environment as they began their life together. Paris added a dimension of excitement and sophistication that would influence the course of the rest of their lives. Their fortunes were determined not by the stars, as they often believed, but by the convergence of extraordinary people, places, and events during the early years of the 1920s.

CHAPTER 2

Paris and Love

The glorious years that Rosemary remembered began for her in Paris in 1920. As a twenty-one-year-old graduate of the University of Chicago, she was beginning to prove her writing skills in the international world of journalism, writing for the European edition of the *Chicago Tribune* after working on smaller publications. Her success came easily to her; the story of Rosemary Carr's early life sounds like a young girl's fantasy of what growing up might be. Bright, healthy, beautiful, and popular, she seemed to find no obstacles in achieving whatever she wished. Born in Chicago on January 14, 1898, she was declared a beauty by anyone who mentioned her. Her fair skin, dark eyes that were luminous and penetrating, and slender body were among her distinguishing features. Throughout her schooling, she was studious as well as academically talented; a friend at Hyde Park High School wrote to ask, "Please don't study so hard. It makes me nervous." She was admitted to the University of Chicago at seventeen, where achievement in her study of French, Latin, and English led to her election to Phi Beta Kappa in her junior year. At the same time, she was popular among her peers, who chose her for the best sorority and elected her "Prom Leader," an honor important enough to be mentioned in the alumni news two years after her graduation. A decade later her mother still sent her information about a college sorority called the Esoterics, whose members remained among her closest friends.

After graduation Rosemary taught in Janesville, Wisconsin, briefly but apparently effectively—one student, Clea Bysted, wrote, "Honestly, Miss Carr, I love you," and added that she was losing weight and crying every night because of Rosemary's departure. But Rosemary had become the first American to be awarded a fellowship to study at the École Normale

Supérieure de Sèvres, a training institution for teachers in French colleges and lycées. On September 23, 1919, she sailed for Liverpool on the RMS *Orduna*.

In spite of what she called her "well ordered convent existence" at the École, Rosemary enjoyed most of her time at Sèvres. Attendance at the opera, visits to Paris museums, and trips to the French countryside provided pleasant breaks from her studies, which she generally enjoyed, with the exception of philosophy. "Art may be long—but philosophy is *interminable!!*" she wrote to her mother.[1] She refused an opportunity to study at the École for a second year because she thought that life there was too protected, and besides, she had no ambitions to become a professional scholar or to remain in France. Some of her observations show that she was not entirely enchanted with French culture: the treatment of the elderly, the occasional disdain of her classmates for American life, the "spoony couples" in public, some of whom she described as forty and ugly, all distressed her. Her intention was to return to Chicago at the end of the academic year or perhaps to find work in France for only a few months.

In the meantime, the frequent letters between mother and daughter were full of information on both sides and much advice on Dr. Carr's part. She recommended red wine for a friend's digestive condition and kept Rosemary up to date on American politics—the steel strike in November, the ratification of the League of Nations, President Wilson's illness, and the deplorable quality of the party candidates. Early in the spring she wrote about Thomas Carr's health, which had lately become problematic. In spite of a heart problem and low blood pressure, he had been taking Turkish baths, which she advised against, along with more stimulants than she was aware of. His doctor's opinion was that he would recover slowly. The most frequently repeated refrain in all the letters was anticipation for Rosemary's return to Chicago.

But Rosemary's life in France was changing rapidly from a convent-like routine to cosmopolitan excitement. First, friends arrived from London for a visit and showed her the Paris that they knew well—charming shops, studios of artists ("delightful, cultivated ones[,] not the long-haired variety"), and delicious cakes and tea. The newlyweds were the former Alice Lee Herrick, nicknamed Slee, and Richard Myers, who Rosemary declared was "a dear and very congenial, if impractical." The couple quickly introduced her to the exuberant circle that would soon dominate her social life.

When they returned to Paris that summer to live in a flat owned by the musician Douglas Moore, Rosemary enlarged on her opinion of Richard: he was the most amusing person she had ever met, but it seemed a shame that anyone so charming would probably be a wretched husband. He had no money sense and loved "a good time which can't be paid for by song-writing which is his talent. Isn't it a pity that you can't find both qualities in one man—which is why I'm single still, as it were!"[2] Rosemary's estimates of people were generally accurate, but she had yet to learn the many qualities of the remarkable Richard Myers, who would become a force in her life.

To begin, he introduced her to William Francis, a newspaperman whose wife wrote the Paris column for *Vogue*. Through them Rosemary met Catharine Hopkins, a young American expatriate artist who also worked for *Vogue*, doing illustrations, mostly of children, animals, and plants. She also designed the paper dolls published by the *Delineator* that were so popular in that period. In the early twenties, she was mentioned as one of the important American illustrators living in Paris. At the end of the school year, Catharine found a part-time job for Rosemary at *Welcome*, a magazine for Americans abroad, and on the basis of her work, Francis offered her a job with the Cross-Atlantic Newspaper Service. In January 1921 she joined the staff of the European edition of the *Chicago Tribune*, writing theater and fashion reviews, some signed "R.M.C."—"(Me!)," she boasted to her mother. At the *Tribune* Christmas luncheon given by Colonel McCormick, the paper's owner and publisher, she was in such high regard that she was seated to the right of Floyd Gibbons, the European director; the wife of Colonel McCormick was on Gibbons's left and was very cordial to Rosemary. Gibbons wrote a glowing letter of appreciation when Rosemary left the employ of the newspaper.

The more lasting result of all these arrangements was that Rosemary and Catharine became fast friends and soon shared a bright, comfortable studio apartment at 8 rue de la Grande Chaumière. Catharine, whose social connections were notable, knew the owner, who was, according to Rosemary's account, "one of those artistic birds, without being an artist, and wealthy which helps so much with taste. We don't like to think what he had this studio for, but there's no use worrying about that because in Paris one can't be too particular and after all, we do mail him cheques for the rent."[3]

Their neighbors included close friends of the Myerses, Douglas Moore and his wife. Moore, like Myers, was in Paris to study with Nadia Boulanger. His sense of fun and his devotion to his friends helped make the Paris years exciting for the group surrounding him. He and his new bride, Emily, welcomed Rosemary into their lively crowd, which knew well how to enjoy the pleasures of being young and living in Paris in the twenties. One member of that crowd was Stephen Vincent Benét, who interested Rosemary because of his intelligence and sense of humor. That he was an established novelist and poet was an added attraction.

Stephen was born in Bethlehem, Pennsylvania, on July 22, 1898, and grew up in a military family that moved often, notably to Watervliet, New York, and later to Benicia, California. His interest in literature began very early. Legend has it that in spite of some damage to his eyes from a bout with scarlet fever, he read a translation of Dante when he was five. Unidentified pains often confined him to his bed, where he read books from his father's library. He arrived in Paris as the recipient of a fellowship granted by the faculty at Yale. Both the students and the faculty in the English Department respected him, in part because he had already published a volume of poetry, *Five Men and Pompey*. Douglas Moore remembered years later that Stephen "came in like a whirlwind" and was immediately accepted into the Elizabethan Club, a prestigious literary group whose members at the time included Philip Barry, Thornton Wilder, and Archibald MacLeish. Beyond his poetic talent, his geniality and infectious sense of humor made him well liked by nearly everyone he met. Many of his classmates at Yale remained close friends and supporters throughout his life.

After graduating in 1918 and being rejected by the army because of his poor eyesight, he briefly worked for the Department of State in Washington and then in an advertising agency; neither desk job pleased him, and he soon returned to Yale to earn a master's degree, with a volume of poetry substituting for the traditional thesis. His literary successes earned him fellowships, first at the college, and then for support that allowed him to travel for study and writing. On August 28, 1920, he sailed for Paris. He stayed with his uncle, Laurence Benét, at an elegant apartment on the avenue de Camoens when he arrived and maintained that as his address even after he moved to bachelor quarters with American friends Henry Carter and Stanley Hawks.

When his brother, William, arrived in Paris while Edna St. Vincent Millay was visiting, Stephen joined them in their pleasures in the city. Other friends already in Paris, in addition to Douglas and Emily Moore, who lived nearby in Montparnasse, were two other musicians, Quincy Porter and Bruce Simonds, and an architect and artist, Don Campbell. Stephen reported to his friend Ethel Andrews in New Haven that they were all working or playing with much avidity, and he joined in both activities. In spite of the fact that Paris was full of liquor, amusing people, and incredibly beautiful works of art, he managed to complete a novel, *The Beginning of Wisdom*, and begin another, *Jean Huguenot*, during his first year in Paris.

Stephen liked to work in Douglas Moore's apartment and was invited to the parties given by Alice Lee Myers. They amused themselves by devising clever costumes, singing, and playing charades. One diversion of this literate group was writing letters to the Paris edition of the *Herald Tribune*, new on the scene and willing to print their contributions, which were usually satirical and even nonsensical. Moore recalled Stephen's defense of a bad piano performance by a friend: "What could have been more or less impressive than his rendering of Chopin's grand old Funeral March?"[4]

At a party in November 1920 the lively group included an interesting young writer described by Douglas Moore as "a wonderful combination of shyness and sedateness, fancy and irony, and lovely to look at."[5] After only a few weeks it was apparent to their friends that Rosemary Carr and Stephen Benét were to become a couple, but Moore had some persuading to do before Stephen would feel worthy of the courtship of the young beauty. He was so diffident that he may not have recognized an overture by Rosemary, but she had taken the initiative early in their relationship when she tracked him down in the University Union at the Sorbonne to ask about a poem. She then included him in her party invitations. His letter to his mother in December mentioned the "most amusing" *réveillon* party at the apartment shared by Rosemary and Catharine, and it was clear that he had already told his family about meeting Rosemary. She, in turn, had begun to mention him in her letters to her mother, asking if she had read any poetry by Stephen Vincent Benét: "He is plain, large, bites his fingernails, but is too smart for words."[6] When Rosemary informed her mother that Stephen's father was a brigadier general—a funny combination, she thought—Rachel was confused. His father never reached a rank above colonel; his grandfather was the general.

In January Rosemary wrote an extraordinary letter that revealed so much of the turmoil she must have felt, far from her family and among new people whom she called "those highbrows." Then there was the question of romance; she confessed that Stephen, under the influence of too much punch, had followed her about at Moore's recent party, discoursing on her hardness of heart.

> He obviously thinks he's in love with me. . . . As long as he lends me books and writes poetry to me, I think it's delightful—and he has too much sense to go further. He is the most companionable person I've ever known, I shall never fall in love with him, and he, being a poet, will probably change his mind about me next week. He calls me Jane, because of a delightful poem we found about a practical little girl, who demanded crumpets and jam and a ride on a bumpity wagon of hay when some romantic gentle man offered her pink pomegranates and love in mist or something like that.

Stephen's new name for Rosemary came from Walter de la Mare's "Bunches of Grapes."[7]

In describing the "highbrow" Paris crowd, Rosemary nevertheless said that she really loved that group of people. Her roommate, Catharine, she added, was much more critical of the others, finding them less complete; Rosemary thought that it was because Catharine's nature was so complex but added that she was so lovely and fine, in most ways doomed somehow to unhappiness and disappointment because she analyzed so much and was sensitive. She was blind to the faults of those she adored and merciless to the others. This—almost a prophecy of Catharine's future—was one of Rosemary's many extremely perceptive descriptions of the people she met in Paris. She had already assured her mother that Catharine's background was respectable: she came from a substantial family, her father had made his money in the World's Fair, her mother was a Christian Scientist, and she had no intention of ever returning to America. An earlier letter had revealed that Catharine must have had an independent income; one clue was that she wore designer clothes, mostly Lanvin.

As for Rosemary's own accomplishments at the time, she feared that her bright ambitions had not been realized:

> I'm no genius, but know too, that you'll love me anyhow. All people love their mothers, but not everyone can feel as I do, a pride and admiration in all you've thought and done. This somehow sounds silly in words,

but I'm trusting to your intuition to get my meaning—and you've seldom failed me there. For whatever our differences are, we've always
had a bond of understanding appreciation that I find as I get older, is
rare. You've no idea the comfort it is to me, when people misjudge me
(either for better or worse) to think that you know all about me and still
have confidence in me. It is a pretty shining thought for me.

As she often did, she asked her mother not to show the letter to anyone:
"This is just between you and me—a sort of heart to heart talk which I
needed infinitely."[8]

Perhaps she was beginning to recognize the separation that would
soon come, even while denying it to herself. But besides attending the
many parties with their friends, she began to meet Stephen for lunch,
often at Prunier's and other popular restaurants. His almost daily letters
now addressed her as "Jane," lamenting when he had not seen her for two
days and noting that she wrote very nice letters.

At the end of January Rosemary made a promising career move to the
Paris office of the *Herald Tribune*. One reason, no doubt, was that she had
proved her abilities at the lesser publications that she had been writing
for, but promises by Stephen's Aunt Margaret to keep her informed of
the doings of the smart set must have influenced the decision about her
hiring. Her writing career may have been a remote consideration in her
attraction to Stephen the poet. "I can't believe I can ever fall in love with
anyone. I am terribly fond of Steve and admire him and am congenial
with him; and that ought to be enough." But she did think about his influence on her as a writer, since all of his family were writers—not, she
added, that she should consider that in her choice of a husband.

The more interesting news to her mother on February 27, however,
must have been that Stephen had written some poems about Rosemary.
She enclosed seven of them, all well-crafted verses that were worthy of
inclusion, with very few changes, in the *Selected Works of Stephen Vincent
Benét* more than twenty years later. Her explanations revealed her tenta-
tive feelings about the developing relationship:

Here are Steve's poems about me—all but the last of which I have no
copy.

Please tell me what you think of them *critically*—for I count on your judgment and shall be terribly interested in what you have to say. *Don't*, I beg, *read them to people* who might misunderstand. Steve simply writes poetry about what is nearest to him—quite naturally & unaffectedly—and we have seen a lot of each other this winter and are the best of friends.

He is an extremely charming person in lots of way [*sic*]—as sweet in nature as he is unattractive outwardly.

The poems are full of clever allusions to lovable animals and the natural world, all related to Rosemary's appearance and temperament. The first one, "Names," contrasts the beauty of hers to the ugliness of others: "But your name is a green small garden, a rush asleep in a pool." God "gave you a name like sunlight, and clover and hollyhocks." "A Cheerful Song" tells her: "Wake! And wash your lily skin / Brush your elvish hair / And then go put the sunlight in / The whole large air!" "A Keepsake Song" is in praise of Rosemary's laugh: "Whether she chuckles like a dove / Or laughs like April rain / It is her heart and hands and love / The moth-wing soul of Jane." "Difference" contrasts Stephen's mind with Rosemary's: his is "a country like the dark side of the moon"; hers is "water through an April night, / A cherry branch, plume-feathery with its white." Rosemary told her mother that the poems were "much too nice to be I, of course, but I love thinking I inspired anything so whimsical and imaginative." The poems soon appeared in *Vanity Fair,* the *New Republic,* Ainslee's *Smart Set,* and the *Bookman.*

A letter soon afterward describes Stephen's imagination and sense of humor but tries to reassure her mother: "This sounds as though I were much more interested in him than I am. I just mention him because he is the first poet I ever knew, and they are so apt to be diverting personages." She sent photographs and letters that told of the holiday parties with the people she called her best friends in France, but she must have felt the need to convince Dr. Carr, and perhaps herself, that her primary attachment was still to her family.

Rosemary's letters to her mother contained other news: she and Catharine had gone to Alice Lee's on Sunday, they had lost their studio and had to move, Catharine had finally started sketching for *Vogue.* She omitted the information about Catharine's affair with Condé Nast, the publisher of that magazine. It may not have seemed important at the time, since her friends took her many affairs lightly and Nast had not yet become a problem. Besides, Rosemary's own developing romance posed a problem. In addition to poems, Stephen was sending her flowers, and soon she realized that he was in love with her and that she did not know how to respond to the new circumstances. She did not believe he had enough money to ask her to marry him, but she was uncertain and unhappy with matters as they stood. She thought at that moment that she would come home in June. Then on March 17 the problem seemed to be solved: "We are just good friends again, which I like—Stephen having forgotten that he thought he was in love with me in the excitement of making money. Just like all men—success is a so much bigger game."

Either Rosemary had read Stephen's intentions badly or she wanted to avoid alarming her parents. She met him for dinner that St. Patrick's Day, and the next morning he wrote to her by *pneumatique,* the small notes carried by the postal service that were their daily means of communication even though they met on most days. "I want to poke myself to make sure that I'm real," he wrote. "It is too incredible & wonderful." They had kissed for the first time and declared their love. The next day he wrote, "We *will* be married in November."

They waited for some weeks to communicate their news to their families. Rosemary wrote to her mother and sent a letter by Stephen in a separate envelope, hoping that both letters would arrive together. But Stephen's was the first to reach Chicago, alarming Dr. Carr enough that she sent him a reply that same day: "Your letter of early April came to me this afternoon & has filled my thoughts since. To say it was wholly unexpected would not be true, for Rosemary's letters told consciously and unconsciously how large a part you were having in her life since she has been in Paris." Their happiness was important to her, she said, but she was depressed by the thought that Rosemary would not live near her. Further, she reminded him that the couple were young and untried, and there were long years in the future. She concluded in a formal, rather distant, tone: "I am deeply grateful to you for your many kindnesses to Rosemary & trust that you will continue to befriend her and send her back to us in June that you and she may have a few months of quiet and separation in which to question your hearts. Do write to me again. I may be clearer-headed the next time and better able to counsel with you."

Rosemary's letter reached Dr. Carr the next day, and again she replied immediately:

Yesterday April 15 came Steve's letter & today your letter of March 31st & its announcement of your engagement to Stephen Vincent Benét. While I have realized the large place he has had in your life in Paris, yet I was surprised at the news of your engagement & I find when I look back that I had been hoping nothing definite would bind you while in Paris. After thinking the situation over, I am convinced you should not make definite promises. You are away from your home, out of your normal surroundings, more or less at the mercy of your feelings & it may be a little home-sick. All I wish you to understand is that the conditions are not normal for making so important a decision. These same objections apply to Stephen Benét. . . . I am asking you to postpone a final decision till you are both in your own surroundings in the midst of your families, & under the guidance of those who love you & wish you well. It quite upset me to think of your walking the streets of Paris to find companionship possible. This must not be, and do give Mrs. Meyers [*sic*] my gratitude for coming to your aid.

We wish to have you come home as soon as you can make your arrangements. Your father joins me in this request.

Enjoy Mr. Benét's companionship & be grateful to him for his kindnesses to you, but remember how much he may be in need of a chance to study the situation & to change his mind if he finds it is best for him.

You both have my deepest wishes for your welfare & it is this that prompts me to ask you to wait till you are normally situated before fully deciding your future. With much love, I am yours devotedly.

Thomas Carr wrote to Stephen on the same day, echoing Dr. Carr's words:

In acknowledging your recent letter, permit me to say that Rosemary's mother has written fully touching the subject presented and that her expressed views are mine also. I have no other inclination than to think well of you, and note future developments. You are of good family, have educational honors, are evidently well bred and so entitled to credit and respect.

I have long wished Rosemary to return home and do not regard her present environment as suitable for important decisions to be made.

Her work has doubtless been informing and she has met good people; however I wish soon to see her here where in the security of her own home in normal surroundings she can be her natural self.—With good wishes. Believe me.

The young people, reluctant to postpone their plans, acceded to the demands of the Carrs. Stephen's second letter of April 5 to Rosemary complained, "It will be the devil when you are in Chicago and I in N.Y. but worth it. Il faut souffrir—I suppose."[9]

Letters from the Benét family to Rosemary were immediate and cordial. "They seem to have unlimited faith in his judgment," she told her own wary parents. But she wondered at the tone of her future mother-in-law's welcome: "Isn't his mother like a sister or a girl in her attitude?"

The situation was still tense on May 18, when Stephen wrote to his friend Shreve Badger, announcing the coming wedding and asking him to be an usher, but demanding that he keep this a secret because his fiancée's family did not approve. But both lovers wrote apologetic letters to Rosemary's parents, and more cordial and welcoming responses eased the strain by the end of May. Dr. Carr, however, was still annoyed because she had not been able to announce their engagement before the Paris friends had done so. Stephen made plans to leave the last of June on the *Aquitainia* but finally sailed on the *Lorraine*. When Rosemary arrived late in New York aboard the *Saxonia* on July 15, they briefly met, carefully chaperoned by Dr. Carr, who had been warned by Rosemary, "Everyone loves him here. Make a few allowances at first for surface queerness and I know you'll see what a gentle, sweet, lovable person he is underneath."[10] With just time enough for another good-bye, they then departed, he for his parents' home in Scarsdale and she for hers in Chicago.

CHAPTER 3

At Home

Stephen moved into his parents' crowded and chaotic household in Scarsdale. Colonel Benét, just beginning his retirement, had to settle for a home far from the place in Benicia, California, or the South Seas that he had hoped for. The suburban residence was a decided downgrade from the commandant's headquarters to which the family was accustomed. In addition to the colonel and his wife, Fanny, the household included their daughter, Laura; eighty-seven-year-old Aunt Agnes; and the three young children of William Rose Benét, who worked in New York but was often in residence at Scarsdale. The house had recently been named the "Brimming Cup." Somehow, they found a room for Stephen and a "tin hell of a garage" where he could work. In July he wrote to Rosemary, "Our present mode of living is intimate to say the least. We are crowded into the house like sprats in a seine and have no servants. Consequently I dry dishes, split kindling etc." His father, he said, was magnificent—"Belisarius in his old age running a vacuum cleaner." But he was happy that his family all had a sense of humor, although his mother despaired at times, wondering if she would be setting tables in Hell. William also complained in his letters to Elinor Wylie about trying to help out, although he escaped for a month during the summer to write at the MacDowell Colony. Stephen declared that the only luminous moment of the day was when Rosemary, William's youngest daughter, yelled into Aunt Agnes's ear, "Under the bridge," which "nearly scared the old lady into a nervous collapse."

Nevertheless, he finished the revisions on his new novel, *Jean Huguenot*, and began to write some short stories. He confessed a "dreadful secret" to Rosemary: "The reason I am as far along as I am at 23 is not due to genius or inspiration or anything one-millionth as pleasant—it all boils down to a certain fluency with language and more than that by several cubits and kilos another certain ability which I feel I ought to take a considerable Moral and Christian Pride in being able to sit down and work when I don't feel like it. And that is not being modest to have you compliment me, really—that is verité [*sic*]."

But the truth was that he was given much encouragement after his friend John Farrar introduced him to Carl Brandt, one of the leading literary agents of the time, who had already been recommended to Stephen by the playwright Sidney Howard in Paris. Brandt immediately recognized the talent that should be developed. Knowing that Stephen needed money in order to be married, Brandt offered advice on the kinds of fiction that would sell and his assistance in placing the completed work with the right publisher. He became a mentor and a friend, in several ways the architect of Stephen's remarkable career.

His frequent letters to Rosemary in Chicago that summer were filled with information about his writing, the publishing prospects, tidbits about the household ("Our sixth cook has left"), and most of all long passages of endearment to his bride-to-be. But there were problems occasionally. William's son, Jim, and Mrs. Benét were both ill at the same time, with no competent help to care for them. Jim was diagnosed as having "walking typhoid," requiring vaccinations for the entire family. Stephen had difficulties with hay fever ("I am an Animated Sneeze") and a nasty doctor who could only recommend a trip to Cape Cod for a month ("I love certain species of doctors—they are so Really Helpful"). And he was seriously concerned about his brother, although he did not put the details in his letter. William was recovering from two great losses. His wife, Teresa, had died in the 1919 flu epidemic, leaving him to care for their three children. Then, Henry Hoyt, William's close friend from Yale with whom he had shared a New York apartment, had committed suicide the following year. And just now William had fallen in love with Henry's sister, the poet Elinor Wylie, who was still married to her second husband and living in Washington. She had not yet told her mother or her husband of her intention to marry William. To make matters worse, the Benét parents concealed none of their disapproval of the affair, and Stephen was often in the middle of the controversy that would disrupt the peace of the family for years.

Rosemary worked that summer in the recorder's office at the University of Chicago, but the job had no claim on her interest. Her social life was hardly more exciting than her job. She described a gathering of the Midland Authors that she attended: "The meeting was too funny for words—most of the ladies old and a bit queer—dowdy I should say if the word weren't cruel. And no one has ever heard of most of those who attend regularly. The distinguished ones stay away." She did note that the poet Harriet Monroe was small and attractive and had a delightful voice. Rosemary received a gracious welcome only because someone thought her mother was a delightful person. After that evening, she considered possible escapes from her boredom.

She proposed taking a teaching position in Scarborough, where she and Stephen might be able to see each other often, but he rejected the idea quickly; a nine-month commitment would mean that they would not be married before June of the next year. She then thought she might like to go to Paris with her friend Ruth, but he explained that he now had two books ready for publication whose sale would allow them to be married in a few weeks, when they could go abroad together.

Rosemary wrote lovely long letters to Catharine Hopkins in Paris, keeping up to date on the events there and supplying her lovelorn friend with information about Condé Nast's activities in New York. He had written to Catharine in July telling of his delight in Rosemary's visit but then had sent no letters after that. Catharine behaved like an adolescent where he was concerned, swimming as far as she could out into the Atlantic off the coast of France, for example, in order to be closer to him in the United States, and, imagining that he was in Newport, also swimming in the ocean at the same time ("the same ocean you know and all that").[1] She was also grateful to Rosemary for visiting the Hopkins family in New York, where Lydia Hopkins found her "charming & wonderfully poised and sweet with little-girl eyes." Rosemary found the family not as "different" as Catharine.

By October Stephen's confidence in his new earning powers was confirmed. He proposed a plan offered by Carl Brandt: instead of spending a year in Paris as they had planned, they should be married very soon, spend three months abroad on their honeymoon, then return for further promotion of Stephen's work. Later they would be free to return to France. Sure of her reply, he ended with, "Well, my letters from now on may be full of boats and licenses and things. . . ."[2]

Their undated November letters did discuss such things as steamer rugs, but two apparent virgins about to be married that month had postponed some more important discussions. Rosemary agreed with Stephen's decision in his earlier letter:

As you say, it would be much better if we should not have any children for a while—much oh much. They would be such an interruption and a bother and would tie us down so. And I hate being tied down!! Also they would be such a nuisance and expense. I don't want them now and it is unfair to them to have them and not want them very much. (This all sounds curiously involved & formal—& them used impersonally like that, suggests triplets at least. But you know what I mean even if I do sound cold & horrid & calculating.)

Then twenty-three-year-old Rosemary, who had been living with her doting physician mother for four months, wrote, "You find out about Birth Control because there doesnt [sic] seem to be much way that I can." That request can be explained only in light of the sexual mores of the early twentieth century.

Stephen's reply was practical:

I'm enclosing Dr. Stopes [sic] "Wise Parenthood" in this and another letter, having finally managed to get hold of it. I was going to send it with its cover on at first but the mail takes so long and is rather uncertain with packages and besides I thought it might a trifle embarrassing if opened in public under the impression that it was a wedding-present. I've read it and it seems pretty sensible—most people seem unable to write about sex without making grand vague allusions to the Life Force and Beauty of Unfolding Womanhood in the manner of Dr. Frank Crane but this lady doesn't, which pleases me. The idea of having children for the benefit of the Human Race has somehow always made me perfectly wild. Any children we have we'll have because we love each other and them for ourselves—not for some blasted capital-ized abstraction—and I bet they'll be able to push these Eugenic Babes all over the lot, mentally, morally and spiritually. . . .

We've never talked particular [sic] about what idiots call "the physi-cal side" of being married—they'd call poetry "physical" because it was written with a pen—but then we've never had to. . . . And oh Jane Jane Jane it would about have broken my heart dear if I'd spoiled anything of what marriage will be to us in the tiniest way before I knew you.

Stephen had to notify his friend Shreve Badger that he should report to Chicago on Saturday, November 26, to be an usher; the others whom he asked to be his groomsmen were Henry Carter and Stan Hawks, his roommates during his early years in Paris. His brother, William, as best man, would be the only member of the Benét family present. The "fairly small" but formal ceremony was held at St. Paul's Episcopal Church, and the reception was at the newly built Versailles Hotel in Chicago. Stephen liked the pleasant coincidence of the "shift in scenery from the Café Versailles to the Hotel Versailles."

In William's autobiographical poem, *The Dust Which Is God*, he described Rosemary at this time; he knew from others, he wrote, of her "cleverness and charm and clear shining," but when he met her, he was entirely captured by "her smile amused, affectionate and shy; her clear blue eyes and roseleaf skin, straight slimness, and little quirk of laughter at the corner of mouth and eyes."[3] Rosemary, at the beginning of the feminist twenties, had skipped the flapper stage and immediately assumed the characteristics of what the *New York Times* called the new siren of the Champs-Élysées and Park Avenue: "European in her poise, her knowledge of clothes and of the uses of mystery, American in her clear beauty of slim form, her calm directness, she is an enchanting proof that the Old and New Continents, when they work together, can do better than either of them alone."[4] Rosemary's experience in Europe had helped to equip her to be the beautiful, sophisticated wife of a man who was to become an American legend.

The couple traveled immediately to New York in a drawing room aboard the *Twentieth Century*. The rest of their honeymoon was meticulously planned by Richard Myers, still the bon vivant that Rosemary remembered, but now the manager of the advertising department of American Express in Paris. Her early fear that he would be an impecunious and unreliable husband for Alice Lee had been far from the mark; his success and affluence only increased through the years, and his friendship and remarkable spirit constantly brightened the Benéts' world. As he kept them informed of events in the Paris that they loved, his letters captured the tone of the twenties in their exuberance and wit. On hearing of the coming wedding, he wrote, "I am saving a delicious bottle of very old champagne for you, which we shall all drink together at 21 rue Visconti," the Myerses' address in Paris.[5] His new position and his own travel experience provided information for three pages of detailed recommendations for a grand honeymoon, including train schedules, important sights, hotels, shops, restaurants, and of course wines. The itinerary started in Paris and led to Marseilles, Menton, Cannes, Genoa, Florence, Siena, and Rome. He arranged for the American Express Company to provide the tickets for the journey.

On arrival in New York, Rosemary wrote to thank her parents for the wedding. She also needed to apologize: "I'm sorry I got cross sometimes for I love you both and shall miss you both and home very much in spite of having Paris and Stephen to console me."[6] By December 8 they were aboard a ship of the White Star Line, one not altogether to Rosemary's liking. In spite of Stephen's earlier warning that they would have to economize on their honeymoon, she wrote, "I do hate second class in spite of my best efforts not to. That is, my fellow passengers. In general first class fraternizes much more than second—By the second day out in first class you know lots of people but here everyone seems a bit suspicious of his fellow passengers. However, I am not sorry really that I do. Stephen and I have not concentrated our attention on the passengers, I admit."[7] On the twentieth of December they were back in Paris, ready to follow Richard Myers's delightful directions, which started: "Leave Paris from the Gare de Lyon at *8 A.M. SHARP*. Arrive Marseille at 9:30. An autobus from the Hotel Splendide will be waiting at the station."

CHAPTER 4

Marriage and Families

On January 13 the newlyweds reached Menton. To her family Rosemary wrote about the scenery—the most gorgeous she had ever seen. They drove to Nice and climbed to Eze, a walled mountain town. After a visit to Monte Carlo, Stephen was eager to move on to Italy, stopping at Florence and Rome; he promised Rosemary a trip to London and the English countryside in exchange before they sailed for home. They clearly followed the Myerses' itinerary. As much as Rosemary enjoyed the trip, she feared that she was a poor traveling companion; she was tired and depressed—a result of the grippe from which she suffered and undoubtedly the reaction to the excitement and stress of planning for a sudden wedding. Although she seldom mentioned depression in any of her letters, she was to be subject to bouts at stressful times throughout her life.

Family and friends kept in touch during the honeymoon trip. Richard Myers kept up his supervision of their travels ("Please write and tell us how you like Menton." "While you are in Italy, you must not drink any of the ordinary water. Order Sangemimi." "Be sure to write me before you start for Rome.").[1] The elder Benéts kept them informed about the home front. Aunt Agnes wrote, "I think, dear Stephen, it was the first Christmas you had not been one of the family circle." She was wrong; he had been in Paris during the 1920 holidays. Laura wrote a chatty letter praising the "wondrous" *Moby-Dick*, a novel newly rediscovered by the literary world, and she was busy writing an article about Herman Melville. She described the holidays in Scarsdale, especially the generous gifts of Kathleen Norris, William's sister-in-law, and her husband. January, Laura said, was a real family affair—the birthday month of five family members, including Teresa, William's late wife, and now Rosemary. Family was the very strong theme of those letters. On Rosemary's side of the family, Dr. Carr's letter on April 11 sent word that Papa was looking better and accepting his debility, but his tremor was now more pronounced.

Richard Myers met the newlyweds for their departure from Paris and then kept up his gossipy letters. Alice Lee, his wife, was away, and Catharine, Rosemary's former roommate, was trying to console him by taking him to wicked haunts like Maurice's. The sidewalks of Paris were so full of Americans that he had to walk in the street. Catharine had decided not to see Condé Nast anymore—"serial number of this decision No. 35679922." Catharine's affair with Nast had gone on for some time, at least as far back as May 1921, when Stephen wrote Rosemary, "I see Condé is now watching the porpoises and probably composing long steamer letters to Cath." That affair was a greater problem to her close friends than most of her other romantic alliances, and her infatuation with Nast, married and a notorious womanizer, continued for years. As for Stephen and Rosemary, Richard promised, "I shall be waiting at the Gare St. Lazare when you arrive in September—n'importe quelle heure."

On their return to the United States, the couple first visited Stephen's family in Scarsdale, where Rosemary enjoyed the company of William's daughters, Rosemary and Kathleen Anne. Stephen wrote to Dr. Carr that Kathleen Anne was "enormous," but Rosemary's letter told her mother only that both girls were more darling than ever. The family in New York attended poetry meetings, and Laura gave a tea for Stephen and Rosemary at the offices of *Broom*, a magazine where Lola Ridge, an influential liberal writer and a Benét family friend, was editor. Many celebrities had been invited for the affair.

By June the couple had separated once again. Rosemary hurried to Chicago to see her increasingly feeble father, while Stephen stayed in Scarsdale to write short stories for the popular magazines. He was patterning his stories after those written by Edna St. Vincent Millay as Nancy Boyd and Elinor Wylie as Nancy MacMichael for *Vanity Fair*. Although he was trying to set aside some time to write poetry, he often interrupted his work to scour the areas around New York City to find suitable quarters for them upon Rosemary's return, finally locating an apartment at 326 East Fifty-seventh Street. And a serious family matter increasingly demanded his time: William's plan to wed Elinor Wylie in spite of her current married status caused much family anguish. The tenor of meetings between

Mrs. Benét and Elinor ranged from tense to hysterical, and Stephen became his mother's reluctant confidant. He confessed to Rosemary, "I must either laugh or frazzle myself to pieces." Mrs. Benét's report that Elinor's mother wanted her to remain celibate for the rest of her life moved him "to laughter akin to weeping."[2] In support of William, and because he genuinely admired Elinor's talent, he tried to maintain some neutrality, even after her vicious review of his third novel, *Young People's Pride*, when it was published in 1922. But his job was difficult; Laura disliked Elinor intensely, and the colonel referred to her only as "the lady in question." All saw her as a potential threat to the family, especially where the future care of William's children was concerned.

Elinor had another conflict that kept her in a bad mood, one that involved William's sister-in-law, the famous novelist Kathleen Norris. William and Kay, as she was called, were still very close, although it had been three years since Teresa's death. Kay loved the children and had a sense of family at least as strong as the Benéts'. But in more than eighty novels she considered everything around her as grist for her mill. For her recent novel, *Certain People of Importance*, she included the names Stephen and Fanny, which no one seemed to notice. But she also included Nell (and Nelly), names for Elinor used by both her mother and William. The character is "as innocent as a butterfly." This would have caused no problem, except that Kay's next book was *Butterfly*, a devastating attack on an Elinor look-alike, "an extraordinarily thin, frail, polished little bit of humanity," beautiful, seductive, and bloodless. "The exquisitely flawless face, under its visible films of powder, rouge, and paste, the lips stiff with brilliant paint, the bright hair scalloped into curves of marble firmness, the eye lashes lightly freighted with some black oil, their surrounding sockets touched with faint lavender shadows— it was all like something machine-made, finished, dressed in laces and gold brocades, hung with sparkling jewels, and sent forth to be admired. And the woman's soul within; that was the same."[3]

Elinor was distressed about the novel before it was published, writing to William from the MacDowell writers' colony in 1922 that all might be well with her "if only I can keep my temper about having to lend my looks to a certain well-known lady novelist." *Family Gathering*, Kathleen Norris's memoir published thirty years after Elinor's death, describes her in only slightly gentler language, although the two writers maintained civility when they were in each other's company as part of the extended Benét clan.

Another source of difficulty, which would have been a minor problem for almost anyone other than Elinor, was John Farrar's important literary luncheon given each year in his capacity as editor of the *Bookman*. John was a friend whom Stephen often depended upon for professional favors at many critical points in his career. As William's friend, too, he knew Elinor and had published a few of her poems. He earned her wrath by inviting Stephen to the luncheon that year and omitting her. In an undated letter to William, she wrote, "Why does this miserable young rat not desire my presence at his damned teaparty?" William was helpless to try to calm her as she dubbed Farrar "the Virgin Queen" without any basis in fact for the title.

In the midst of these controversies, both major and insignificant, Stephen must have felt frustration when reading the letters from Richard Myers, as delightful as they were. They reminded him that he hated the New York literary scene; Rosemary, too, wanted to be in Paris, where the best of friends were waiting. They had barely arrived in the States when Richard wrote, "The gang no longer exists—Catherine [*sic*] and us—that's all. You *must* come back. To say we miss you is uttering a worthless platitude. It is positively disheartening to come home at night and find the salon empty and the divan in perfect order. I no longer discover hairpins in the grand piano nor long golden hairs in the bonboniere [*sic*] and I can't get used to not hearing Rosemary's careless and ultra-casual remarks—intimating what a perfect stranger you are to her."[4]

Now this summer he asked again, "When are you coming back?" His letters were full of news about Paris people: Laurence and Margaret Benét were in the news so often that he thought the reporters had a standing order to print something every day; Catharine was trying to live within her income, and Richard hoped that C. Nast would stay away (there was a strange story to be told about that gentleman); he had a letter from Douglas Moore that was so delightfully naughty that he carried it everywhere; the entire colony had read Rosemary's latest letter with pleasure; one woman who asked if Rosemary had been a bad influence on Stephen's work was told that he was writing better than ever. He described a Paris dinner given by Sidney Howard's mother: "The other night we had melon—*filet de sole Foyot, poulet en casserole a la reine, pommes soufflés—peches a la cardinal* [*sic*] or some damn old rip—and well—I won't go on! Yes I will because it might bring you back sooner—the wines were a light and elegant Meursault and rich and imposing Burgundy. We finished off with fine old Courvoisier brandy of 1850. And—when do you think you'll be back?"⁵ Stephen had already decided when he wrote to Rosemary before their marriage that they were going back, "sink or swim, live or die, survive or perish!"

Carl Brandt, however, had persuaded Stephen that he could be much more productive if he stayed close to his agent and publisher. Stephen was producing the short stories that provided his main income, but his aversion to writing popular fiction was apparent. He wasn't alone in the literary world in his dislike of writing stories only for money. F. Scott Fitzgerald wrote to Maxwell Perkins, his editor, "I now get $2000 a story but I hate like hell to do them,"⁶ and Elinor Wylie told a friend that writing a short story for a popular magazine was an ordeal she never again would undertake. Benét's own struggle with the need to write short stories is mirrored in his novel *James Shore's Daughter* by a narrator with an artistic conscience who resists an inferior plan: "It wasn't so bad, in itself, but I knew it was the thin end of a wedge . . . something puffy and second-rate, like a boiled Brussels sprout, with the cabbagy taste of petty knavery about it."⁷ Only later, after the period when he had to tailor the stories to publishers' requirements, did Stephen's genius find its way into short fiction as well.

In August, Vachel Lindsay, a poet much admired by Rosemary, visited for a weekend. "He was delightful," she told her mother. The family was rather quiet for a change: Laura had taken young Rosemary and Kathleen Anne for a vacation in the country, and William was away. But Mrs. Benét was having problems with her vision, which one doctor diagnosed as glaucoma, recommending an operation. Not until December did she find a physician who promised that the progress of her disease could be retarded without surgery. One cheerful bit of news was that Elinor had been sweeter to everyone lately, and the family seemed resigned to William's affair—all except the colonel, who remained, according to Rosemary, "obstinate and aloof."

The good news from abroad was that Alice Lee Myers had delivered her second child, a blond boy with blue eyes. Richard, who kept everyone up to date on Catharine's many love affairs, feared that she would probably steal the beautiful baby boy from under their very noses. She had had several recent proposals, but he said all were too young for her. In a letter to Rosemary, who liked the New York writers even less than did Stephen, he agreed, "From all accounts the younger literati are rather disappointing. I hope they don't take the bloom off Stephen's genuine naturalness.

They are all so *important!*—aren't they?" Then he teased her: "And the couturiere sales commence tomorrow. Poor Jane."[8]

In early December William's three children, Jim, Rosemary, and Kathleen Anne, visited on what their Aunt Rosemary told Dr. Carr was one of the most hectic days of her life. After they toured the toy shops, Rosemary made lunch, took them to visit a great-aunt, and prepared a "tremendous tea." They were sweet children, she said, but by the time they departed on the 6:19, she was a wreck.

As the holidays approached, Rosemary was a little anxious: "We haven't been out to Scarsdale for a week, but we will go there on Christmas. There has been great speculation as to whether Elinor Wyley [*sic*] was or was not to be among those present but the last word is that she is invited."[9] In the flurry of Christmas parties, Elinor gave her own in her apartment at University Place; in attendance were William, Stephen and Rosemary, and the Colums, the poet Padraic and his wife, the writer Mary. Elinor spent Christmas day for the first time with the Benét family in Scarsdale then hurried away early in the evening to be at a party given by John Dos Passos in New York.

CHAPTER 5

Complications

Rosemary and Stephen celebrated the New Year of 1923 with the Andrews family in New Haven. John Andrews was Stephen's classmate and close friend, and his sister Ethel was a friend of both Benéts. Their father was Charles Andrews, a Yale professor of history who had taught Stephen in one of the few classes that he attended regularly. Ethel was later married to Supreme Court justice John Harlan.

The newlyweds were living on Fifty-seventh Street. The other members of the Benét family at the still "Brimming Cup" were ill with the grippe. The colonel had been confined to bed for the first time in forty years; Laura's infection was the worst, recurring for a second bout; and the children coughed all night. William had been stricken suddenly at Elinor's apartment, and the doctor, he told the family, had kept him there. Stephen was well but worked at both helping William and calming his mother, who had "lost her head entirely." Although she had the assistance of a full-time nurse, she was convinced that everyone was going to die. To her mother, Rosemary observed, "I can't help feeling at times that the excess of emotion is rather selfish." Stephen, she said, "remains calm, keeps his head and is a mountain of tact with everyone concerned."[1]

The bright spot that week was news of the *Nation*'s prize for Stephen's "King David" as the best poem of the year. It was praised by poets such as Edgar Lee Masters and John Drinkwater, but condemned by others as irreverent or even obscene. Colonel Benét wrote to advise his son, "Why not try to write moral literature. Pure sweet literature such as our people love. Try, try."[2]

Another of Stephen's important poems of that period was "The Ballad of William Sycamore." Along with "King David," it marked the moment that he found his voice, which defined the American nation at the time. Among the few sour reviews was Edmund Wilson's in *Vanity Fair*, calling the poem doggerel and referring to Stephen as "that bright comet of the *Yale Literary Magazine.*" To make matters worse, Wilson praised his friend Elinor Wylie's second volume of poetry, *Black Armour*, in the same column. He had in fact just hired her as a part-time editor at *Vanity Fair* after she contributed several poems to that magazine. Probably the preeminent critic of the twenties, Wilson, a Princetonian, was accused by William of being unfair to Stephen because he was a Yale man, and also of being jealous of Elinor and William's relationship.

Rosemary was excited to see Catharine's picture and one of her sketches in the January 1 issue of *Vogue*. On January 22 she wrote to thank Catharine for sending her, anonymously, a beautiful dress. She reported that she was looking for a cat, but since she had decided to name it Catharine Hopkins, she had not found one worthy of the name that she could afford. Twice in that letter Rosemary asked about Condé Nast:

> How is Mr. Nast? Are you as fond of him as ever? He lives at 58th and Park Avenue, I hear, and I always hope that I shall bump into him, sometime. But I suppose he would be in a large town motor, so I better take out accident insurance before hoping. I should love to see him, though, especially if he has any news of you. Elinor Wylie, who may be part of our family ere long, and is already a sister to me, is most enthusiastic about Mr. Crowninshield [editor of *Vanity Fair*]. She says that he is most clever and delightful about the office, and that it is great fun working for him. However, I always say that Mr. Nast is much nicer, I am sure.

Rosemary apologized for the "disgracefully long letter" but added, "But I pine for news of you all and Paris. . . . Oh you are lucky to be there and I wish we were too. . . . We are coming back as soon as we get any money, or enough money, which God willing, I hope will not be far away."[3]

Rosemary met two interesting women writers in January at a dinner given by John Farrar. The novelist Mary Austen, she said, was "an extraordinary looking woman, a little eccentric, but good hearted, I imagine. She is devoted to the interests of the Indian and thinks they have been hardly and unjustly treated. She also told us a wonderful ghost story." Of Amy Lowell she wrote, "She is a brilliant conversationalist which is fortunate as she talks all the time. She reminds me of Dr. Van Hoosen in voice, expression and build. She is very *very* stout and smokes cigars, but has a delightfully keen mind and very fine intellectual face. When William spoke at Wellesley he visited Miss Lowell in Boston where she has a wonderful house all full of rare books. An amazing person!" Rosemary added two bits of personal news: Elinor had promised to try to find a job for her at *Vogue* or *Vanity Fair*, and with the Benéts all recovered from their illnesses, the nurse was leaving.

Mrs. Benét recovered enough to write to Dr. Carr about the household, reporting that the colonel had had bronchial pneumonia and William had low blood pressure and a high temperature; his nerves were "shaken to bits." She left it to Rosemary to tell her mother that even the spectators of his two-year-long fight over Elinor were getting very edgy. Her kinder words were about the children. Kathleen Anne grew more beautiful by the day, Rosemary was developing into a bookworm, and Jim loved books and movies.

In February, when nothing had come of Elinor's promise to find her a job, Rosemary applied for an interview at *Vogue*. The "lofty lady" who asked her about her background was impressed by her clippings and even more because Rosemary was married to a brilliant writer and personally knew both Frank Crowninshield, the editor of *Vanity Fair*, and Condé Nast, the publisher of *Vanity Fair* and *Vogue*. She was hoping for some work to do—something more interesting than housework, she said, especially if Stephen would be writing continuously on a new novel. The need for money must have been another reason she wanted work. Elinor had started to present her with clothes and perfume that she could not afford. She could not refuse, she told her mother, because Elinor took a childish pleasure in giving the gifts. And Richard Myers must have inadvertently hurt her when he wrote from Paris, "I saw the new Lucille collection—and Oh Jane Rosemary—I thought of you—you dainty little sophisticated Dresden china shepherdess. There's a dress there that shouts for you—two of them in fact—you must have them. Shall I buy them when the sale comes off? Or will you be here."[4] He must have realized what Rosemary's response would be when he wrote on April 15, "Premet's are selling a gown for 675 francs that looks like Rosemary! (That was mean of you, Dick!)"

In fact, Rosemary was making over some of her dresses from high school that summer, she told her mother. Her other topic in the same letter was an old one. "Elinor, William and the Benéts have been having a great to-do lately, and I am tired of hearing about it. We get both sides, as we are strictly neutral, and the result is that we are hearing pros and cons most of the time. . . . Elinor is certainly very delightful and fascinating, and one can't condemn her unheard, though I am sorry for the rest of the family who disapprove." Aunt Margaret in Paris had joined the fray with gusto, declaring that "Wm. is in the clutches of the most unscrupulous & brazen creature that ever lived. . . . As I see it, it means a very deep & lasting sorrow to his father & mother & one I fear that will estrange Wm. from them & all relations & friends."[5] The socially correct Aunt Margaret so often reinforced Richard Myers's opinion of her—that she was all right, "just a least little wee bit conventional and slightly touched with ignorance."[6]

Mrs. Benét made a strong overture toward peace with Elinor just at this time, forced by developments in the affair. The preliminary papers for Elinor's divorce from Horace Wylie came through, with the final decree due in October. Almost simultaneously the newspapers announced the engagement of Mrs. Elinor Hoyt Hichborn Wylie to William Rose Benét. As a veteran military wife, Mrs. Benét must have recognized a lost battle. In a letter to Elinor she suggested, "Let us look to the future and be patient with each other," and confessed that she was not at all proud of herself. But the main point of the letter was what would happen to William's children. Of course they would have to be with him, and therefore Elinor must be a mother. But, she said, "darling Rosemary" notes that they "need a lot of loving." The elder Benéts proposed that William and Elinor take their house so that the children would be in a familiar environment. Hoping that these matters could be resolved once Elinor returned from her summer at the MacDowell writers' colony, Mrs. Benét closed with a most conciliatory "Goodnight, my dear—All my desire is to 'be friends' & to be understanding & true with you—Believe me."[7] She signed her letter "F.R.B.," not "Mother Bunny," as in her letters to Rosemary.

Stephen was busy with his usual writing projects, as well as reviews for *Time* and two plays, *The Awful Mrs. Eaton* and *Nerves*, in collaboration with John Farrar. During the tryout period for *Mrs. Eaton*, Stephen and Rosemary had been in Cleveland, where Douglas Moore was musical director of the Cleveland Museum. Together again, they resurrected the playful spirit of the Paris days, creating an evening of "Polyphonic Poetry," which Moore declared was the latest French artistic movement. The poems were followed by "formidable lectures on the poetical and musical issues involved." As Moore described the event thirty years later,

> the theory was that poetry had now reached the stage when a single line no longer had meaning and verses should be combined in the contrapuntal manner to reveal new beauties. Steve wrote a polypoem which was supposed to combine the ultra masculine with the ultra feminine point of view. The masculine one began, "Son of the North, the North am I whelped in a forest where werewolves cry—Woof." At the same time the feminine poem, read by Rosemary was going on, "My soul is like a cockle shell, a wee small thing with a fragrant smell." The audience was not entirely convinced as to the artistic merit of the movement, except for some of the musicians who said that this was really an important idea.[8]

In spite of Stephen Benét's successes, both popular and critical, with the exception of a few years, he continually struggled to earn enough just to maintain a meager income. As he once wrote to his mother, "Darn the money thing, it makes me so annoyed." But the free books and theater tickets that came with Stephen's reviewing job pleased Rosemary.

That spring Rosemary enclosed clippings about Elinor and her family with her letters to her mother. Pictures of Elinor and Edna St. Vincent Millay appeared in *Vanity Fair*, and the "Mad Hoyts," as they were named by gossip columnists, appeared often in the news, more because of their outrageous behavior than their prominent social status. Now Elinor's younger sister Nancy had scandalized Washington society by canceling her lavish wedding the night before the guests arrived, some of them from London, where the groom's family lived. Nancy's romances and marriages were followed faithfully by reporters, who used fiction as well as fact in their stories about the Hoyts. Nancy was the youngest and her mother's favorite; Rosemary said that her behavior must be very hard on Mrs. Hoyt, "although she must be inured to surprises by now." Always conscious of her position as a grande dame in the Washington world, she announced, "I have given birth to a generation of vipers." The affair eventually quieted, but the periodic bursts of publicity annoyed the elder Benéts. With one clipping, Rosemary commented that every child in the Hoyt family had had a scandal, including Morton, whose wife had run away with another man the year before. That wife was Eugenia (Jeanne) Bankhead, daughter of Senator Bankhead and sister of Tallulah, the movie actress. Morton and Jeanne's first marriage in 1918 had been annulled at the insistence of the senator; the second took place in 1920 in Bar Harbor.

In April Alice Lee Myers traveled to New York with her two children. Catharine, who had resigned from her job in Paris at *Vogue*, accompanied them, along with Monty, her wire-haired terrier. Also in April Kathleen Norris, her husband, Charles—or Cigi, as she called him—and William's children traveled to Chicago, hoping to see the Carrs for the first time. Rosemary helped to shop for the children's trip. "I am glad Mrs. Norris is to meet you, as she has been so nice and cordial to us—in fact, even harboring no resentment towards Elinor," Rosemary wrote to her mother on April 23. She was a "very charming and big hearted woman with a delightful sense of humor, never shown in some of her cheaper more popular novels. . . . She must be a little like Theresa [*sic*], William's first wife, for she has her fine carriage and height."

Although the meeting in Chicago did not take place at that time because of a late train, efforts were continued to connect the Carrs and the Norrises, as well as the Benéts and the Hoyts. Extended family members and even college friends formed bonds that created a large community, demanding contact, communication, and care, even when there was no great affection. In each of these often difficult relationships Rosemary frequently took responsibility for setting matters right, or at least calming the aggrieved parties. The summer of 1923 offered a little respite.

One help to Rosemary was Catharine's arrival in the United States and her decision to live permanently nearby. Soon afterward Rosemary had lunch with the Hopkins family. Rigid Christian Scientists and prohibitionists, they seemed the antithesis of their flamboyant daughter; only the grandmother could be described as charming. Catharine preferred to live near the Benéts and soon moved to 41 Washington Square South. As usual, she had many admirers, and when one gave her a case of champagne and gin, Rosemary was pleased to send a bottle of gin to her ailing father; she chose the gin—"the good before the war kind"—because it would last. Champagne, she said, must be opened and taken down at one gulp. In May, Rosemary, Catharine, and Frieda, her sister, visited the Benét family in Scarsdale.

Elinor soon escaped both the scandal of her sister's aborted wedding and the disappointment of her own short-lived job at *Vanity Fair* to stay in residence at the MacDowell Colony in Peterborough, New Hampshire. The colonel, Mrs. Benét, and Laura left in June for a long vacation in Nova Scotia. Laura, perhaps most of all, had suffered emotionally from the fracas over William's wedding and even more from the knowledge that Kathleen Anne, Rosemary, and Jim would be taken from them to live with Elinor and William. Mrs. Benét often fed Laura's anxieties with her own complaints. Her Uncle Will, Mrs. Benét's brother, wrote to her that summer, "I hope you can lay aside authorship for a time and build up your shattered nerves and health."[9] An accomplished writer who would later have many books to her credit, Laura was fragile both physically and emotionally at this time. Like her father, she never was reconciled to Elinor's presence and could not even admit that she had talent. Laura's refusal to admit that Elinor was beautiful enraged her sister-in-law even more.

Rosemary was also worried about her friend Edna St. Vincent Millay, who had been ill with what was termed alcoholic gastritis. She recovered long enough to be married to Eugen Boissevain, a wealthy Dutch importer, then went immediately to the hospital for an operation. Rosemary wrote to Dr. Carr, "I hope they will be very happy because Edna is an extraordinary person. I can't imagine her married, though, and indeed she loudly said that she never would and is one of the least domestic geniuses I have ever seen."[10]

Just before Elinor left for her summer residence at the MacDowell Colony to finish her book, she and William came to dinner, along with Catharine and Don Campbell, a friend from Yale and the Paris days. Rosemary breathed a sigh of relief as she told her mother that she and Stephen were left lonely but at peace. With time for herself, she attended a reunion of former classmates; none of them, she regretted, were her favorites. On Fifth Avenue in New York she met F. Scott Fitzgerald, who recognized Stephen and stopped them on the street. In August they planned a vacation at Amagansett, hoping that Catharine, who also needed a break, could join them. Otherwise, Rosemary was not interested in meeting many people. She told her mother that she dreaded the time before Elinor and William's wedding, which was set for October, and asked for the name of a woman doctor in New York. After a number of delays, the Amagansett visit left her sleepy and hungry and relaxed. She feared that the delicious state would not last long, because the Benéts were probably going to arrive en masse in September, having rented the house until the fifteenth. The colonel would not be with them, since he had decided to visit his brother Laurence in Paris until after William's wedding. Rosemary explained to her mother that he was "under a great strain here from a situation of which he does not approve and this allows things to adjust themselves."

Mrs. Benét had to stay to take care of Aunt Agnes and probably the children until after the honeymoon. "It is really going to be a very difficult time, and we all wish we could get away from it. It is especially hard for me as Elinor tells me all her woes, and I feel like a hypocrite whatever side I take." Rosemary also reported in the same letter that Constance, Elinor's sister and the family beauty—Horace Wylie had called her the most beautiful debutante ever to come out in Washington—had died. Married to a German diplomat, she was the Baroness von Stumm. Rosemary stated that Constance had died suddenly of a heart attack, and if she knew of the stories of an unhappy love affair and suicide, she did not tell her mother.

The Benéts returned from Nova Scotia on September 8, the children looking very well and Mrs. Benét very fat. The colonel had already sailed for France on the SS *President Adams,* refusing to let anyone see him off, and Elinor was in Washington. On September 19 Rosemary revealed the reason for her request to her mother for a doctor's name—she was pregnant. She was a little worried because she had no nausea, and Dr. Glasgow had said that she had anemia and low blood pressure and that her cervix was "out of place." Stephen's letter to Dr. Carr the same day told of his hope for the future: (1) blue eyes, (2) curly hair, (3) female preferred— in fact, as exact a replica of Jane as possible. He promised to choke off the stream of people visiting or calling at all hours—"especially Elinor, who when she's temperamental would make a wooden figurehead nervous, let alone an ordinary human being."

Rosemary found that Elinor had been "weeping out her woes" on Catharine's shoulders, an imposition, because she did not know Catharine well at all. But Elinor wept for anyone who was at all sympathetic. For the coming wedding Dr. Carr sent a handkerchief to Elinor, who found it exactly right as a "something blue" to carry. Elinor added, "Rosemary has been so perfect a friend that now she is to be a sort of sister I feel a very special kind of satisfaction. She is a wonder child, as pretty as a flower & as dependable as a rock. It is very rare to find charm & integrity so beautifully joined. I truly love her, & if I have ever been kind to her, I have only repaid her invariable kindness to me."[11] Rosemary's note at the top of the page identifies the letter: "To my mother, thanking her for a small present—this was sent me by mother later, because she knew how I would treasure what she says."

On her part, there is no doubt that Elinor's admiration of the woman she called "Darling Ro," was unqualified. But Rosemary's feelings were made increasingly complicated by Elinor's erratic behavior. While the Benéts were away, at one point she could report that Elinor had been behaving beautifully, but suddenly, in the middle of Grand Central Station, she became very emotional, probably because William had forgotten her for a moment as the children were leaving for California, and she was not the center of what was going on. Catharine saved the situation by laughing at her and saying she was childish. That had a magic effect, Rosemary said, and Elinor at once behaved. "But we were completely floored, and poor William! I felt so sorry for him. I began to wonder again how it can possibly turn out." But in spite of family disapproval, she and Stephen gave a dinner party for the couple, inviting sixteen people, including Franklin P. Adams, columnist for the *New York World;* Esther Root, his future wife; and John Dos Passos.

On October 5 the ceremony was held in the Fifty-sixth Street apartment of Elinor's friend Claire Mumford. A Unitarian minister who was an admirer of Elinor's poetry was, in Rosemary's words, "willing to officiate, in spite of the blots on the scutcheon which might trouble the soul of an Episcopal minister." The bride and groom were "radiant and beaming," and she looked about twenty. The wedding was charming, Rosemary said, but then, as Catharine remarked, "When we are having our third weddings we will know how to do things, too." Rosemary added, "I doubt if the finger of our sins will fall as lightly on us as it seems to on E. Wylie." The poet Amy Lowell arrived with her companion, Ada Russell, after the ceremony and reportedly congratulated the bride then added what was either a strong threat or a weak joke: "But if you marry again, I shall cut you dead—and I warn you all Society will do the same. You will be nobody."[12] Mrs. Benét and Laura came and departed swiftly after the ceremony. "They were very brave about it, but nevertheless looked like figures of woe and mourning all through it." Catharine, telling Richard Myers that she felt like a society reporter, listed the rest of the admirers in attendance: "Franklin P. Adams, Don Stewart, John Dos Passos, John Farrar, Frank Crowninshield, along with a poetry club, editresses, poets, and poetesses *ad infinitum* were there."[13]

There was a great deal of confusion about both the bride's and the groom's attendants. Rosemary told her mother on October 1 that Stephen would be his brother's best man, and Catharine's letter to Richard after the wedding verifies that; yet Stanley Olson's biography of Elinor says that it was F. P. Adams who served in that capacity, and Nancy Hoyt's memoir says that she supposed that "F.P.A." was Bill's best man. Esther Root was Elinor's bridesmaid. The question of the bride's choice is clear because Rosemary reviewed it in detail for her mother:

> At the last moment, she asked me if I would mind letting Esther Root, a bovine celebrity collector whom I do not like, stand up with her instead of me—as "she had set her heart on it like a child." What could I say, but accept, although this was two minutes before the wedding and she had asked me to do it a week before? Of course I said it didn't matter at all, but I am still frightfully hurt, because I realized as soon as Esther came in, that it must have been arranged the day before, as she was all dressed and ready for the part.

Nevertheless, Rosemary enjoyed the ceremony and seeing her many friends.

Elinor's mother and sister were not invited, her sister Nancy says in her memoir. Neither was Elinor's friend Edmund Wilson, who noted in his diary that it would be a pity "that a first-rate poet should be turned into a second-rate poet by marrying a third-rate poet."[14] James Branch Cabell, another friend, noted in his memoirs that Elinor "had found, after marrying several of them, that this world was full of disappointments."[15]

Colonel Benét, seething in Paris, wrote to his wife the next day:

> As this is the 6th, I suppose that the inevitable has happened and that the sacrifice has been consummated. What will the end of it be? I cannot think of any thing we could have done to prevent it. We were once a united family and now however much we may try we can never be. An instance of the Vanity of Human Wishes—come to grief. I hope they will take the children as soon as possible and finish up this scene of the drama. If it is to be done, the quicker the better. It will yield less pain. But the pain is inevitable. I carry a heavy heart when I think of it all—a load of trouble that will last till I die. It will require all your fortitude and patience to carry you along through this but at our age time passes

rapidly—that is one comfort. And perhaps you will be too busy to be able to think much.

In reply to Stephen's letter describing the wedding, he wrote, "I was delighted to get your letter so clearly written. I confess the Unitarian service rather staggered me. As she had to go to another state to get a divorce, evidently she is not divorced in NY but Wylie's wife still there. This being the case, how can she be married in New York? . . . For your mother and sister the ceremony was a crucifixion. But they were present and satisfied the conventions." But he feared the worst that awaited Mrs. Benét was the giving up of the children. The colonel was prescient here: "The lady I know does not want them but William will force her there I think. I don't think she will be able to squirm out but will probably show him practically after a month or two that the situation is impossible. Poor William, he has much ahead of him! . . . Now that they are married we shall have to recognize her, but we may as well admit it, this breaks up the family. William quite naturally will not be satisfied unless we show as much affection for her as we do for Rosemary and that is impossible."[16]

Even Rosemary and Stephen wanted some separation from William and Elinor after the wedding and all the turmoil leading up to that event. The family tried to evade them for as long as possible that fall, but the inevitable hard trial that the colonel feared for his wife came on November 8, when Laura took the children to a New York apartment on Eighteenth Street, where Elinor and William first lived.

November found the scene relatively peaceful. Stephen and Rosemary visited William and Elinor and declared that the children were adapting well and William was radiant. "The rest of the family are almost disappointed at the smoothness of the installation after their predictions of failure," Rosemary told her mother. Again at Thanksgiving, after a luncheon with John Farrar and his mother, dinner at the William Benéts' was pleasant, with what Rosemary thought was an excellent cold turkey and potato salad made by their German cook.

The children, who called Elinor "Missy," had begun to dislike her as they coped with her headaches and tantrums. After the next fall, when they moved to New Canaan, Rosemary recalled that Mrs. Benét and the colonel never saw Elinor or wrote to her. When Laura came to visit, Elinor left the house before her arrival. Rosemary, the younger daughter, remembered that Elinor bought them beautiful clothes that they disliked, a tea set too expensive to use, and a dollhouse too perfect to play with. "Living with Elinor was like walking through a flowery minefield," Rosemary Benét Dawson recalled.[17]

In Chicago Dr. Carr was in danger of losing her job with the insurance company because the firm had been sold to owners who had a medical advisor onboard. Rosemary wanted to help but had to admit that she and Stephen were unusually poor that year. "I do think money is the *most* unfair thing in the world," she told her mother. There was Elinor, who wanted sympathy because her allowance from the Hoyt estate was too small and she had to sell her second-best fur coat. "It's too mean!" Rosemary wrote in an uncharacteristic complaint. But there were even more serious problems looming. Thomas Carr's condition was deteriorating to the point that his behavior sometimes annoyed Dr. Carr. He had begun to interrupt her as she examined patients, and she could do little to control him. Although his physician had just said that the problems had been developing over a long period, Dr. Carr continued in her insistence that her husband could do more to improve his health.

With Stephen, William, and the children gone from the Scarsdale house, the colonel and Mrs. Benét moved to the Huntington, a boardinghouse in Kingston, New York. Mrs. Benét was reading Elinor's first novel, *Jennifer Lorn,* and found it fascinating and beautifully done, she told William. She said that she was pleased to hear that Frieda, his new cook, was such a treasure, but he must have tried to put the best face possible on the situation or else his standards differed from his younger daughter's; she remembered years later that life was difficult for everyone, compounded by the fact that Frieda, the German cook who was apparently all they could afford on their budget, was not very skilled and insisted on having her dachshund as a family member. And further, she was not very fond of children.

Rosemary was prodding Dr. Glasgow, who was now interested in electrotherapy and no longer treated pregnant women, to recommend an obstetrician for the birth of her child, expected in four months. When Mrs. Benét and Laura heard of the pregnancy, they annoyed Rosemary by saying they had both dreamed about it: "It is *so* silly and they keep harking back to the vision. Besides, as I told Stephen you simply cannot surprise people like that no matter what you do." Mrs. Benét insisted that the baby would be a boy.

William's children were spending part of the holidays in Kingston, but the mood was not one of celebration. Laura's despondence at losing the children was made worse by the rejection of her novel by two publishers. The colonel was still in Paris with his brother Laurence and Margaret, although he soon found the Paris winter cold and sailed for home in late December. Christmas brought a crisis when Kathleen Anne contracted diphtheria, requiring Elinor and William to be quarantined and Rosemary and Stephen to be vaccinated. Dr. Constance Guion, who was Elinor's physician as well as her friend, came to treat the whole family. By all accounts, Elinor showed her best qualities as she cared tirelessly for "Kit," her favorite of the three children.

CHAPTER 6

Baby

As 1924 began, Stephen continued his collaboration with John Farrar on the two plays *The Awful Mrs. Eaton* and *Nerves*. Expectations were high for the success of both ventures. The colonel arrived home, having thoroughly enjoyed life in Paris. In a letter to Alice Lee and Richard, Rosemary reported that she had quit her pleasant job as reader and editor with the publishing firm of Henry Holt because the conservative culture objected to the "wayward girl in fiction," and she feared that her pregnancy would upset the office morale.[1] But Catharine, who Rosemary declared was partly responsible for this baby because she wanted it so much, was a great help and comfort. Rosemary wrote to Dr. Carr, "Catharine is nicer than ever, if that is possible; I don't know what we would do without her. I pour out my troubles on her shoulder as in the old days, and weep on her antiques when I get gloomy. Her big room is enchanting now; old American things. . . . She certainly has done it all with her usual perfect taste."

Rosemary still was having trouble finding an obstetrician. The one suggested by Dr. Glasgow was unacceptable; she talked only of money. A Dr. Farrar refused her as a patient. Finally, she found a woman doctor, Mary Lee Edward, whom she liked but who believed so strongly in restricting carbohydrates during pregnancy that Rosemary complained that she was eating so many vegetables that she felt like a truck garden. She felt well enough, however, to take a job reading French books for Brandt publishers.

In February Stephen and Laura went to hear Edna St. Vincent Millay read her poetry, during a time when Laura stayed with them while she was looking for a new job. Rosemary told her mother that Dr. Edward said that all was well with her pregnancy; however, soon two cases of scarlet fever were diagnosed in their building, and the doctor recommended that they move out until the threat was over. Dr. Carr did not think it necessary for them to leave and wrote a long letter of advice on avoiding the disease. Nevertheless, they did move to friend's apartment for a suitable period. In March Mrs. Benét came to visit, staying at a hotel nearby. She insisted that she wanted to be present at the birth of Rosemary's child.

Elinor, also pregnant, managed to provide more drama and a family crisis. She was "hysterical with fear and resentment," according to her friend Carl Van Doren in his 1936 tribute in *Harper's*. She had experienced, after bearing a son during her first marriage, three miscarriages and a stillbirth while she was married to Horace Wylie. Continuing to care for William's children was impossible for her as well as for the elder Benéts and Laura, who were living in a boardinghouse, and for Rosemary and Stephen, who faced the imminent birth of their first child. The problem was solved when Kathleen Norris decided to take William's children earlier than usual that year to stay on the California ranch. Rosemary wrote about Kay, "What a diplomat the world lost when she turned to literature! She smoothes the troubled water between the Benéts and Elinor, is in both their good graces, high in their affections and rides the neutral fence far better than I. I marvel at her tact and devotion."[2]

Along the way to California the group stopped in Chicago to meet at last Rachel Carr, who greeted them at the train station. She told Rosemary that Mrs. Norris was big, wholesome looking, and charming. Rosemary insisted that no one felt any resentment toward Elinor in this difficult situation. And after suffering yet another miscarriage, Elinor returned to the MacDowell Colony to begin a new novel, *The Venetian Glass Nephew*. William joined her there for part of the summer.

On April 6 Rosemary delivered a girl, named Stephanie for her father and Jane for her mother. Besides, her poet father said, the rhythm was excellent. Letters describing the birth were sent to Dr. Carr; one bit of information was that Rosemary would be able to leave the hospital three weeks after the birth. "Isn't that fine?" she asked. Another was that neither of the nurses in attendance had ever worked for a woman doctor before. "I didn't realize what an innovation I had started," Rosemary said. The first thing she said to Dr. Edward after the birth was, "Do you think I caused my mother all that pain?" Dr. Carr enthusiastically replied to the letters with much medical advice. Stephen's long, joyful letter to the Myerses reported a healthy baby at seven-and-a-half pounds and asked them to kiss his Aunt Margaret for him—"she must be so relieved to know we have at last done our duty to posterity."[3] Congratulations included a scribbled note from Condé Nast saying that he had intended to call and ask her to lunch that very day.

But just after Rosemary returned home, her appendix ruptured and infection set in after the operation. Dr. Edward treated her, and the baby was removed to a different hospital to be near her pediatrician. Rosemary came home to be cared for by a nurse, a cook, and a maid, but it was some time before she fully recovered. The baby, too, had a setback, but by the end of April her condition was improved. Rosemary's mother, who planned a vacation trip to Windsor, Vermont, in June, decided to stop in New York to attend to mother and infant.

With Rosemary ill and Stephen weary and worried, Catharine wrote to Richard and Alice Lee Myers to bring them up to date about the Benét families. "They are such dears and things have piled up rather thickly upon them," she lamented. She sent news of friends who would call in Paris, one of them Marjorie Pratt, who had an "adorable" husband, Richard, who was an editor at *House and Garden*. Catharine asked Alice Lee to reassure Marjorie "as to my methods with husbands, other people's, I mean. . . . I may be wrong but I think I need your defense of me—However—." Some pages later she followed that cryptic message with another: "I'm contemplating a portentious [*sic*] move. If anything developes [*sic*] I'll let you know." Catharine and Condé Nast had kept their pledge made in Paris not to see each other and now she did, in fact, hope to marry Richard Pratt after he divorced Marjorie.

Rosemary's mother at this time had health problems of her own. Thomas Carr was showing the effects of his progressive disease, never named even by his physician wife; now, instead of using phrases like "Your father is holding his own," she had to confess, in spite of her denial, "I am beginning to think he does not feel things as keenly as he once did."[4] The depression that she felt over his long illness was intensified when she indeed lost her job with the insurance company. In addition, Thomas Carr's sale of prime Chicago property to buy a farm deprived the family of its security. "Decidement [*sic*]," Rosemary told Stephen, "we are not financially a lucky family."

Other members of the extended family were having health crises as well. Aunt Agnes, turning ninety, was so frail that there were questions of how long she could last; she had begun to give away her most beautiful possessions. Mrs. Benét, responding to all the stresses in her life, had what Rosemary called "a kind of nervous breakdown." Nevertheless, the colonel, somewhat oblivious to the conditions of the women about him, said that this was an exciting spring and summer: Rosemary had a new baby, Laura was taking an exam for a new position, William was a principal in the founding of the new *Saturday Review of Literature,* and he and Elinor had a new house in New Canaan.

During that hot summer, Rosemary was grateful for weekend invitations from friends like Douglas and Emily Moore, who had a house on Long Island. At one party, Lola Ridge, the poet and mystic, read Stephanie's palm and predicted that she would distinguish herself as a musician. She also read Stephen's and Rosemary's hands with "amazing intuition." Lola's poetry was filled with a Celtic sensibility, and wrote an entry in her diary and a poem in the *Saturday Review of Literature* in which she claimed to have seen Elinor after her death. There was a heightened interest in the occult during the twenties, and Rosemary and Stephen wrote about their particularly avid interest in astrology. They often presented horoscopes of infants to the new mothers among their friends. Rosemary's clever story "Twinkle, Twinkle, Little Star," published in *Vogue* in 1931, satirized the Parisian rage for the occult.

In mid-September Rosemary spent five days in the hospital for an unnamed malady, and at the end of the month she welcomed Kathleen Anne, Rosemary, and Jim when they returned from California. They came to visit the baby, and Stephen and Rosemary in turn went to see them in New Canaan, where they visited the girls' dancing class and heard part of Elinor's new novel. Rosemary reported to her mother that the children were devoted to Elinor and that New Canaan was a good choice. Stephen and Rosemary, too, had found a suitable place to live but could not afford it. "Maybe we'll be richer next fall," she said. "I have a philosophy like Mr. Micawber fortunately."[5]

Mrs. Benét and Laura came to visit for two days in October. Rosemary told her mother that although Mrs. Benét was very nice, Laura upset her: "She is so nervous and self-centred—that is centred in her family—that I feel no sister-in-law could get on with her—I know the other two, Theresa [*sic*] & Elinor didn't—E. dislikes her intensely."[6] A few weeks later Rosemary felt guilty at her previous judgment; Laura was so often ill and now had a kidney infection. Soon she seemed to be on the verge of a nervous breakdown and actually hysterical. Mrs. Benét's burden was increased, as Aunt Agnes could now hardly see or hear and did not like to be left alone.

The Sunday after Thanksgiving, Rosemary and Stephen went to New Canaan to visit. The dinner was excellent, and the children were smiling and happy. Elinor had written a new poem, "Love to Stephen," which called him a "Cherub in armor; / Wolf in rabbit-skin" and ended:

Perhaps in small ways,
A starched child-chorister,
But fierce, and always
Robin Hood's forester.
Who shall draw
Or tell your story
Brother-in-law
And in outlawry?[7]

Stephen and Rosemary's trials at the end of the year were financial ones. Nevertheless, they enrolled Stephanie in the best kindergarten in New York, the Play School on West Twelfth Street. As winter came, Elinor sent an expensive caracul coat; it was too short, Rosemary said, but very warm. Their poverty, as they called it, contrasted fiercely with the happy-go-lucky world of Paris just four years earlier. It was hard to think about that joyous time, and perhaps that was why Richard Myers wrote from Paris to complain that it had been almost a year since he had heard from them. He complained even more fiercely about Catharine; he had heard rumors about a wedding journey. "To whom and when?" he asked. "That cold-hearted slab of ice hasn't written us for six months. So I've finished with her too. Is America affected by palsy or are writing materials rare and costly?" He reported that he was having tea with Sinclair Lewis, but all litterateurs except Stephen bored him, and Gracie Lewis was a terror. "Come back, Steve," he pleaded.[8]

For Christmas of 1924 Catharine designed a beautiful old-fashioned card with portraits of Stephen, Rosemary, and Stephanie Jane that, for many reasons, they would treasure forever.

CHAPTER 7

Tragedy

Rosemary and Stephen were seeing more people socially than usual, including Carl Brandt; Edna St. Vincent Millay and her husband, Eugen Boissevain; and Vilhjalmur Stefansson, an Arctic explorer and author. At a dinner at the Norrises, they met Edna Ferber, who was "very nice, unspoiled by her success." Rosemary continued to speak of Kathleen Norris as a dear. They gave a dinner party to which Elinor and William, Elinor's brother Morton, and publishers Alfred and Blanche Knopf were invited. At the last minute Elinor wrote to cancel: "As William perhaps told you, Morton was coming on to try to find something to do—write—& I thought he might dine with you. Now I find that he won't go—& Mama won't make him. I think it's silly, but it's none of my business. At any rate, he isn't coming, so none of my family will be there. I'm sorry, & hope it hasn't put you out & that you get this before you order dinner."[1]

One of the most popular novels of 1925 was Michael Arlen's *Green Hat*. Stephen wrote to William thanking Elinor for the green hat she had just sent to Rosemary—"much nicer than Mr. Arlen's." He added that Elinor was a generous angel. The green hat was a fashion item that year, but it had always been a favorite of hers, and there's little doubt that Arlen based much of his novel on the characters and behavior of the Hoyt family. But, as with everything in Elinor's life, it came down to her narcissism. A green hat was more than an item of clothing, as her poem "Green Hair" explains in eighteen couplets:

Now do you wonder that I wear
The hat which I have called Green Hair?
Thus with witchcraft I am crowned

And wrapped in marvels round and round;
There's sorcery in it, and surprise;
Believe your own dark-amber eyes
When mine of hazel look at you
Turned to incredible turquoise blue.[2]

When she came to visit in March, Rosemary was alarmed. "Poor Elinor! She was pathetic." Her blood pressure was 235, and she was very excitable, saying that soon she would not be fit to live with. Rosemary asked her mother how high blood pressure could go. "I am really so fond of her that I can not bear to think of her just working herself off the earth with nervous excitement." Laura, too, was more nervous than ever, but Rosemary did not have the same response to her problem: "I temper my exasperation with her by being sorry for her, but her viewpoint IS narrow, completely limited by her family. However, we are perfectly amicable when we meet. As long as I don't have to see her too often I'm all right."[3]

During a visit to her parents in Chicago, Rosemary sent Mrs. Benét pictures of the baby and Dr. Carr. The absence of the fading Thomas Carr in the photos brought the reply "I hope your father could enjoy Stephanie Jane a little." Rosemary must have recognized even better than her mother his true condition. From that point, her letters home are almost always addressed only to Dr. Rachel Carr. Stephen wrote to Rosemary from New York that he was glad that she would stay as long as she intended—"I have simply *pined* for you all week"—and yet almost as soon as she arrived home, he left for the MacDowell Colony. Just then Minnie, the maid who had been with them since the birth of Stephanie, left, saying she was giving up housework for factory work because of her back. The problem was critical, because those who might replace Minnie could not cook.

Richard Myers wrote to Stephen from Paris, ending with a request to kiss Rosemary and her rosebud daughter for him. He included his habitual complaint about the lack of news from Catharine, suggesting that Steve snub "Corty" for him—or kick her "*exquise derrier* [*sic*]."

In May, Stephen's sonnet sequence "The Golden Corpse" was published in the *Saturday Review of Literature*, newly established by Henry Seidel Canby, his former professor at Yale, and his brother, William. The poem, dedicated to a friend of Paris days, Don Campbell, is among the most accomplished of this period and was highly praised when it was included in

Tiger Joy, with its dedication to Rosemary. The volume contained one of Stephen's loveliest poems to her, beginning, "If you were gone afar."

Stephen, at the MacDowell Colony that year, wrote that he found the company of Edwin Arlington Robinson quite intimidating, so much so that even in his letters to Rosemary he called him Mr. Robinson. The older poet was a kind of reigning king of the colony, spending nearly all his summers there in the twenties. He was very fond of Douglas Moore and William Rose Benét, less so of Elinor Wylie. All three had spent time the previous year in residence there. But Stephen's serious purpose this summer was to have the time and the ideal environment to work on a novel that he had begun in the spring—*Spanish Bayonet*, a fictionalized history of Florida in the eighteenth century, when his Benete ancestors had arrived from Minorca. The family was very conscious of their background, and William and Elinor playfully called them by Spanish names—Esteban for Stephen, Rosa for Rosemary, Pedro for William, for example. These were fond names, in contrast to those Elinor invented for her family, who became the Muscovy Imperial Police. She was sometimes called Dmitri in William's letters and once in a dedication before their relationship was public.

The ending of *Spanish Bayonet* did not please Stephen's agent or the publisher of the *Pictorial Review*, which offered ten thousand dollars for the serialized version of the novel if the author would allow the heroine to live and be romantically united with the hero. During his three weeks at Peterborough, he struggled to write three versions of the conclusion of the story, none of which satisfied the magazine's editors. Stephen's dilemma and his depression over the controversy were not apparent to the other colonists but made him eager to be at home with his wife and daughter. His decision to refuse to go as far as the *Pictorial Review*'s readers may have preferred meant the loss of income for his family, but it reaffirmed his artistic integrity.

The colonel proofread every line of *Spanish Bayonet*, undoubtedly pleased at the military setting and the Benét family connections. He had written a small volume himself earlier in the year and sent a letter to a newspaper to recommend "Mother Truth Melodies," his substitute verses for the objectionable Mother Goose rhymes. His sample lines:

Hey diddle diddle, the Sun's in the middle
Mercury's next to the Sun;

While Venus so bright, by morn and by night
Comes next to join in the fun.

He quoted this to the newspaper from memory, he said, as his own copy had been given to a grandchild.

Elinor, too, was in residence at the MacDowell Colony that year but arrived after Stephen had left. Late in the summer season she wrote to thank Stephen for his volume of poetry, *Tiger Joy*. When the colony closed in the fall, she had not finished her new novel, *Orphan Angel*, and wrote of her concern to Blanche Knopf, her publisher. The children were the problem, she said. She feared that when they returned, "they [would] simply make a sandwich of me and my darling character & devour us. But I am trying to find a way." Soon she wrote to take credit for the solution. "I've arranged with the Norrises about the children." Now, she said, she would be able to work again.[4]

But it was William who was talking to Kay; she offered to "attend to" the schooling of the children—Jim at Choate and Rosemary and Kathleen Anne at a convent—for the remainder of the school year and then to take them with her to California to live with the Norrises permanently. He explained to his mother that there was great stress over money and Elinor's health. Her doctor said that unless she had rest and less worry, it would be only a couple of years before "something bursts." William complained that he hadn't heard from the children, and he longed to see them again, "especially my dear old Jim."[5] Clearly every decision revolved around Elinor's needs, so much so that William's earlier promise as one of the important poets of the time was unfulfilled during the years of his alliance with Elinor. Her corrosive influence was the opposite of Rosemary's encouragement and support of Stephen's talent.

Mrs. Benét was in shock when she learned of the arrangements; it took her several weeks to answer William's letter informing her of them. She wrote to Laura about her hopes that the children might stay in the New Canaan house but added now, "The Norrises with all their money can beat us to the post—for the present but perhaps not always. We shall see."[6] But the senior Benéts were planning to move to a boardinghouse in Poughkeepsie and could not possibly have the children live with them any longer. William was uncertain whether he and Elinor would stay in New Canaan or take an apartment in town.

During this time Rosemary was in New York, where she was working on an editing assignment. But she found time to send Stephen's letters to Peterborough, along with his laundry and a birthday gift for Laura. And of course she cared for Stephanie, who was now at an age where she needed a vaccination and swallowed the beads on her Tinker Toys. "Is there any ostrich in your family?" she asked Stephen. But visits to the woman pediatrician brought some unexpected help: "Docky Pattison knows both of a maid and a luvally apartment with a roof built by an architect."

That summer, however, usually alone with the baby, with little money, an inadequate apartment, and little opportunity to use her own writing talents, Rosemary revealed an edgier side of her personality. She wrote to Stephen that a woman whom he had known in New Haven before he met her had told Elinor that Rosemary was fond of Elinor but afraid of her. Then she added, "Of course that is just the kind of remark that breaks up families." Elinor reportedly answered, "Then why did you say it?" Rosemary reacted in an uncharacteristic, almost adolescent, manner to the hurt, writing for three pages to Stephen "with venom in my pen," then ending, "I don't care if Grace is your dead love, she's a cat." Rosemary sorely needed the presence of her husband and his wonderful sense of humor that deflected her anger and anxiety.

When Stephen came home in September, Rosemary went almost immediately to Chicago. Her father's condition was deteriorating, and Dr. Carr was persuaded to take him to a sanitarium. After four days, she decided that he was not well cared for and brought him home. The weariness of maintaining her practice and caring for him, with only Nellie, the unreliable maid, to help, began to show in her letters of 1925. And with her insurance position gone, money was a problem in that household, too. That month, Dr. Carr's sister died, depriving her of the close relationship she had anticipated for her declining years. When Rosemary returned from Chicago at the end of the month, the family was in the throes of moving to their new apartment at 224 East Fifteenth Street, with enough space for the three of them. Stephanie was growing tall, inventing her own language, and becoming very like Dr. Carr.

On October 9 a heartbroken Rosemary wrote to tell her mother of Catharine's death the night before. Three weeks later she was still reluctant to commit the facts to paper: "Sometime I want to tell you all about it but I can not bear to now. It was a most tragic end." Only later she explained that the thirty-three-year-old Catharine, whose lover, Richard Pratt, was having difficulty obtaining a divorce, had been pregnant. When she started to miscarry from the stress and from other health problems, Dr. Edward had operated. Richard Pratt's position in New York society prompted the newspapers to investigate, and a few carried sensational stories of illegal medical practices. Reporters bombarded the doctor and Catharine's friends with questions, but no cause of death was revealed in print. Even Catharine's mother was not told the truth. Rosemary thought that Pratt was not a knave but a fool and confessed to her mother, "I can't help but be very bitter towards him though I try not to—but it seems to me that she died of cruelty." Richard Myers wrote from Paris, "Darling Corty—so generous, so big and so unselfish. And destined for unhappiness in all her loves."[7]

As distraction Rosemary and Stephen traveled to New Haven, where they saw the Andrews family and attended the Yale-Princeton game. Then they went to tea at John Farrar's house, where Kathleen and Cigi Norris were guests. Several times that month they met with Vachel Lindsay, one of Rosemary's favorites, and his young bride. Richard Myers arrived from Paris, reminding everyone that Catharine had so looked forward to seeing him. Stephen saw him off for France on New Year's Eve, and Douglas and Emily Moore joined Alice and the children in welcoming him home to Paris. Richard had embraced all of the extended Benét family in his ample bosom. He asked to be remembered to "the buoyant Elinor" and said that if Kathleen Norris was coming to Paris soon, he hoped for a note to him—she had sounded so nice that he really would like to know her. He also expressed some of the same disdain that Stephen had for New York literary types: "Oh—that Algonquin! How well I remember it—and the regular habitués—all self-complacency, simply weltering in the egos, and those insufferable dramatic critics!!!! But the pie *was* good!"[8]

Elsewhere there was minor trouble. Mrs. Benét wrote to Laura from Poughkeepsie, where the elder Benéts were living, that she had not heard from William, who was bitterly hurt by a snub from his Uncle Laurence and Aunt Margaret. "They heard in Washington that Elinor was *leaving* William. So you see!"[9] Other people had heard the rumors about William and Elinor; F. Scott Fitzgerald wrote to his editor, Maxwell Perkins, who knew the couple well, "Poor Elinor Wylie! Poor Bill Benét! Poor everybody."[10] Mrs. Benét agreed with him but still tried for an optimistic view: "In spite of stress & struggle, pain, grief & disappointment in 1925, we *have* had sweet joys to compensate, and have been mercifully spared much that might have come."[11]

CHAPTER 8

Paris Encore

At the New Year of 1926 Mrs. Benét wrote to Stephen and Rosemary to tell them of the elder Benéts' pleasure in having William's children with them at Christmas. A visit to West Point to remind them of their family military heritage had been a great success. Stephen was busy helping John Farrar edit a poetry anthology in addition to writing the short stories that provided the family income. His progress was difficult because he had begun to experience severe gastric pains. He submitted to x-rays and complained that his stomach was like an English celebration—so much comment and picture taking. Rosemary was concerned about him and about her parents. Dr. Carr had been sick and had written that she was treated badly by a male physician, while Thomas Carr's condition had not improved and was exacerbated by the cold winter.

Rosemary was still deeply depressed. She told her mother that next to Stephen, Stephanie, and the Carrs, Catharine had been the person nearest to her heart. And now there was no one to whom she could tell her secrets. Soon after Catharine arrived in the United States, she had written to Alice Lee Myers about Rosemary's true emotional state, something that was revealed not even to her husband or her mother: "Rosemary has been wretched & she surely needs to get away from all the literary and at times wearing & boring tea serving & high brow discussions she's had loaded onto her. I think she feels it too & longs to be busy (in her own right). You can't get us old cart horses out of the harness—There's no use trying!"[1] Catharine's death left a permanent void in Rosemary's life. She was pleased only that Mrs. Hopkins suspected nothing of the truth and still talked about the mystery of it all.

In early March Rosemary announced to her mother that Stephen had been awarded the first Guggenheim Fellowship for poetry. A few weeks later she had another momentous bit of news—she was two-and-a-half months pregnant. She still could not believe it; she had hoped for this last fall but was so depressed at Catharine's death that it proved a false alarm. This meant that she would have two children before she was thirty, then she was through, her duty to the race fulfilled. She hoped that Dr. Carr could visit in New York this year so that she and Stephanie would not have to make their annual visit to Chicago. Their last visit had not meant much to her father, she thought. The rest of her letters that April contain only trivial comments. The horoscope her mother sent for Stephanie was better than the one that Rosemary found—"Thank heaven," she added. She was glad that a friend had given Stephanie a new bonnet, because Mrs. Benét had criticized her old one. There was nothing to the rumor about John Dos Passos, and she would see him soon. She asked her mother, "Hasn't the testimony on prohibition been amazing? What a farce it is! I remember your views two years ago—they have certainly been proved."[2]

At the end of March, Rosemary and Stephen attended a party given by Condé Nast for Douglas Fairbanks and Mary Pickford. She told her mother that they both seemed simple and charming. In one letter, Dr. Carr had sent a clipping about Elinor's sister Nancy. Rosemary sent the latest gossip in return: "We hear that she has broken her engagement to the Marquis of Donegal, Earl of Belfast, to become engaged to Henry Carter, a great friend of Stephen's. I'm afraid it won't last, particularly since she is going abroad with her mother and I fear the charms of being marchioness-countess will be too much for her."[3] Jim, Rosemary, and Kathleen Anne came for a visit during their Easter vacation. At the end of April the Norrises took them to California, this time by way of the Panama Canal, to live on the ranch permanently. The Benéts could give much love, but little security or opportunity. With Kay and Cigi, they lived in lavish surroundings with many servants, much entertainment, and superior education. They were well loved by that family, as well as by the Benéts.

In spite of her wish not to travel, Rosemary took Stephanie to Chicago in May, fatigued after a visit from Mrs. Benét. "She is kind, but talks constantly," she told her mother. In New York Stephen wrote "Bon Voyage," a short story that he called "a dear little candy-laxative of a tale." He was sure it would sell—it was so cheap. He had made the decision that they would live in France now that the Guggenheim Fellowship would support the family for awhile, but he told her, "I would live with you anywhere, even in Spartanburg, South Carolina, which is my idea of the nadir of dwelling places." In response to Rosemary's comment about Hemingway—there was gossip in literary circles about a brief romantic episode with Elinor— he said, "I think you're right about Hemingway. But he can write." Finally he added one of his constant love notes: "I think you are the most marvelous and delectable creature under the canopy, not excluding gazelles and phoenixes, in fact I think you are SWELL! I love you. Always."[4]

Richard Myers, greeting the news that Rosemary and Stephen were coming to Paris, took charge, as usual. He asked them to bring two sets of Parcheesi, a popular diversion in Paris at the time; he announced their arrival to Douglas Moore, who would come up from Gérardmer in the Vosges; and he had an apartment ready for them on their arrival. Were they coming on the *DeGrasse?* In fact, they sailed at midnight on July 23 on the *Coronia.* Alice Lee Myers met them at LeHavre and took them to the rue Jadin and comfortable quarters owned by Jean Lamont, a friend of William and the Myerses. For the new tenants Mme Lamont left behind some fine French champagne and, more importantly, her very good French cook. Here Stephanie played in the Parc Monceau and Stephen began work on his long Civil War poem, *John Brown's Body.*

Less than two weeks after their arrival in Paris, they expected that Elinor, who was in England, would arrive in Paris. But on August 8 Elinor sent a note: "I'm not coming. It's because Nancy is thinking of getting married. Not to Donny but to a friend of his, & I have to be in England on the slim chance that it really happens this time." She added that her brother Morton and his wife were with her in London and were reconciled once again. As for her sister's new marital intentions, Elinor wrote, "Don't ask me about Nancy—I mean, ask if you like, but I know no more than you. The young man is good-looking, poor, very poor & a journalist. I believe it is Mama, who, quite unconsciously overturns all these apple-carts of poor Nancy's, or poor Henry's & poor Donny's, & poor Jerry's—not to mention poor Wise-Clarke!" She added that if "Ro" and Stephen wanted to come to be with the Hoyt group, they might come across with Rebecca West and some other free spirits.[5] They declined, choosing to visit Alice Lee and Richard in Bizy, where Douglas and Emily Moore joined them.

William Benét, who had left for the United States in July, wrote to his mother that all was well in California, and that the Norrises were providing the children with all the advantages that they could not have if they lived with him. Kathleen explained that they had decided to stay in California for the winter, because New York was a difficult place to work, and the schools were not appropriate for the children. She offered to pay all expenses for William and Elinor to come to California. In the meantime, William was having difficulties in trying to rent or sell the house in New Canaan.

Upon their arrival in Paris, Rosemary and Stephen had gone to visit the American Hospital to prepare for the arrival of their second child. On September 28 Thomas Carr was born. Rosemary was attended by the famed obstetrician Dr. Bouffe de St. Blaise, a friend of Dr. Robert Proust and his son, Marcel. Rosemary rested in the hospital for three weeks following the difficult birth.

In October Stephen was able to report that Rosemary had written her own "Bon Voyage," a poem that she had just sold to the *New Yorker*. So "tout va bien." The clever poem listed the attractions of Europe for the nine million Americans who had gone abroad that summer. In the British Isles she found

Cheshire cheese,
Hawthorn trees
Prince of Wales,
Nightingales,
Quads and spire,
Seacoal fires.
The Black Watch
(Some hot Scotch),
Coldstream Guards,
Modern bards,
Pope and Milton,
Port and Stilton.

And her favorite things in France included

Cathedral towns
Far and near,
Paris gowns,
Good blond beer.

Crowds at the races,
Chantilly laces,
Paris sun!
Paris rain!

She concluded that, with all this bounty

God's will be done!
I'll see them again!

The *New Yorker* was happy to accept Rosemary's poems whenever she found the time to write them.

Elinor's new novel, *The Orphan Angel,* was released that fall and prompted a letter from Kay to Rosemary: "To tell you the truth I don't like it as well as either of the others." Rosemary's letter to Elinor was very generous, as usual: "It is a miraculous book—worthy of your shining pen. No one else could possibly have done it so magnificently." She added that she was brokenhearted because Jean Lamont needed her lovely Paris apartment at the beginning of the year, and now they must find another. Over Christmas they moved to an apartment in Neuilly, just outside the gates of Paris near the Bois de Boulogne.

CHAPTER 9

Productive Days

The move to Neuilly-sur-Seine, a pleasant Paris suburb, took the Benéts to a comfortable apartment at 89 avenue de Neuilly, which became more acceptable as soon as they removed some objectionable art objects. Françoise, the maid, fainted soon after they moved in, and it took some time for her recovery before the household could be put to rights. But Rosemary slept well here, and Stephen was making headway with his long poem. In contrast to the insufferably hot garage in Scarsdale, his rented fifth-floor writing room had two porthole windows that let the heat escape and made him wish for earmuffs and a bearskin rug. The children were both doing well. Stephanie spoke fluent French, and Tommy was a happy, loving baby, but Rosemary told her mother that they still missed William's children.

By mid-month Rosemary was busy writing a travel brochure for Richard Myers at American Express. She took on many other small projects, such as guidebooks and translations, and she was working on a new piece that she would sell to the *New Yorker*. Stephen's mother wrote to Laura, addressing her as "Pussy Dearest, Darling precious," wondering why Rosemary hadn't written to them, although Stephen and the children had sent letters. They had been in the new apartment for only five weeks before Mrs. Benét came to visit. Soon after her return, the possessions from her former residences, now stored in a warehouse since the move to a boardinghouse, were destroyed in a fire. Rosemary noted that it seemed ironic that the heirlooms should be destroyed after all the years of moving them from one army post to another. It was months before William could assess the damage and help to distribute the remaining items among members of the family. But Mrs. Benét, who set much store by the things in her life, told Rosemary, "I haven't shed a tear. I've no place to shed them. . . . My brain is stupefied."[1] William wrote to say that Laura had been a trooper, and that they had lunched and dined with the Norrises, who had golden reports of the children.

In early March the *New Yorker* took two more of Rosemary's pieces. Her gossip to her mother included the news that Sinclair Lewis, who at Yale had been a close friend of William Benét and Elinor's brother, Henry Hoyt—they called themselves "the three mosquitoes"—was in Paris, and she hoped to see him. Elinor was coming later in the spring, and the latest scandal from her direction was that she had used the money needed to pay for the New Canaan house to buy a letter written by Shelley. Mrs. Benét found more to criticize, as she wrote to Laura about a newspaper clipping: "We see that 'Elinor Wylie, poet and novelist, has sailed for England on the *Paris*.' How underbred & disgusting it is of her to take her passage aboard ship as 'Elinor Wylie'! Her whole attitude is beyond belief."[2]

That outburst did not reach Rosemary, but the news that Nancy had, in fact, left her new husband was abroad. The Hoyts, it seemed, got publicity no matter what they did. That month the *New York World* printed a story about Elinor's paying seventeen hundred dollars for the Shelley letter and twelve hundred dollars for one of his first editions. Rosemary's comment was, "Isn't that amazing? Of course she adores him and her book was about him, but still!! What a lot!" The purchases were actually a letter and a check signed by Shelley, and no amount of money was ever verified. William donated the items to the British Museum upon Elinor's death the following year.

William's children in California had all made their First Communion. Although that was a matter of contention within the Benét family, Rosemary was glad, explaining that it was what their mother, a devout Catholic who had spent some time in a convent, would have wanted. That was probably what Kay Norris was thinking as well. With the children now living with the Norrises permanently, William and Elinor moved to West Ninth Street in New York.

Stephen had gone to Cannes with playwright Philip Barry; although Rosemary had been invited, she said that she wanted to work on her writing. Now that she was back in Paris, she was producing stories and poems again, in spite of the responsibility of caring for Stephen and the two children. The depression that had bothered her in New York disappeared once she found again in France the ambience and the people she loved. Her letters to her mother that spring were filled with mostly happy news. They had found that Tommy would probably be considered an American citizen, since he had been born in the American Hospital. She had previously learned that he could not be president, but she hoped he could be something better. The note included with the enclosed pictures said that he was always smiling. She hoped that John Farrar's young son would be Thomas's friend. She described the marvelous pageantry of the Easter service at Notre Dame, where she found the crowd most interesting. She responded to a clipping that Dr. Carr had sent about the release of Sinclair Lewis's *Elmer Gantry:* it seems, she said, that doctors took *Arrowsmith* in a much better spirit than ministers were taking this; they were making a great fuss over it. And political campaigns in the United States, as usual, captured her interest: "Sorry to hear that Thompson was elected," she said, referring to William "Big Bill" Thompson, the notorious mayor of Chicago. His anti-English policy seemed the greatest silliness, she thought.

William wrote to say that Elinor would be arriving in Paris early in May. Stephen's reply included the information that he thought now that he would call his "thing" *John Brown's Body.* The colonel, who read and critiqued every line, in addition to suggesting ideas and stanzas of his own, found that "And now to see you is more difficult yet" was a vile line, with no music in it. "Go over every line carefully," he warned. Nevertheless, the line remained in the invocation to the poem. Stronger criticism, however, was directed at the very subject of the poem. "Is the epic to be called 'John Brown's Body'? I hope you do not idealize J. B. As I wrote you once before I regard him as a crazy bloody fanatic, rightly hanged. Nothing became him in his life like his leaving of it."[3] As close as father and son were, their attitudes toward people and politics often diverged.

Elinor arrived on the Continent, where she lunched with Rosemary and gave her a beautiful Poiret dress and coat, because, she said, she had bought more than she needed. Rosemary told her mother that it was the loveliest outfit she'd ever had; her thank-you note said, "There is no one like you, dear Elinor, and I remain your admiring and grateful, as well as loving, Rosemary." Elinor declared that Thomas was the most beautiful child she had ever seen and that he resembled William's son, Jim, who had grown into a handsome young man. Elinor's brother, Morton, and his on-again wife, Jeanne, were eager for the Stephen Benéts to attend a housewarming party at 55 quai de Bourbon on the Île St. Louis. Mrs. Benét was up to date on the news and wrote to Laura that Elinor had arrived in Paris and Mrs. Hoyt and Nancy were there, as well as Morton and Jeanne, "so the woods are full of them." Only with Laura did Mrs. Benét link her sharp tongue and her pen, but both women tried Rosemary's patience at times. A letter to her mother tells of her annoyance: she thought that Mrs. B. was truly fond of Stephanie and Tommy, but

> she raves about them in such a sentimental way that it exhausts my response—she says she is "overwhelmed with joy and gratitude that I had the privilege of bringing such little beings into the world," and she has "fallen fathoms deep in love with Tommy. Napoleon is nothing to him nor Alexander the Great. He has the bump of the philoprogenitiveness largely developed and he will only conquer by love not the sword." Imagine that about a baby seven months old! It sounds a little ridiculous to me, proud as I am about them. . . . Not everyone can be a perfect grandmother like you, loving and proud and tender but never silly.[4]

Rosemary was pleased with her household help at the moment. In addition to the children's nurse, Françoise, she had replaced a rather haughty cook, Berthe, with a simple, pleasant Bretonne named Corantine, who was very fond of children and would not mind living in the country, where the family planned to move at the end of the month.

On both sides of the Atlantic the family was excited about Lindbergh's solo flight in May. Rosemary's report to her mother about the event was ecstatic:

> We have all been excited and thrilled by Lindbergh's flight. I don't know when anything has stirred me so. It was such a completely courageous, mad thing to do—a grand gesture. We walked out to get the news late last night and were amazed at the enthusiasm—all the taxi-drivers rushing to buy the extras and crowds milling around. . . . It is nice he has all this triumph while he is so young—and in the face of the gloomy predictions of those who said he was a "Flying Fool."[5]

She thought that anyone else might have been less celebrated in France so soon after the disappearance of the Frenchmen Nungesser and Coli on a transatlantic flight just two weeks before, but no one could feel anything but wonder at this boy.

The excitement was great for some in the United States, as well. The colonel described the attention paid to Lindbergh's return home in his letter to Stephen: "Yesterday your mother who is a Radio Fan and no mistake, sat for four hours at the Radio, intermitting only for a hasty plate of soup, listening to the New York welcome to Lindbergh. She said she was as tired as if she had been at the celebration."[6]

But a letter from Aunt Margaret in Paris, full of the Lindbergh feat at first, stirred stronger emotions that would embroil the entire family for some time. She repeated gossip that William had agreed to allow the Norrises to adopt his children. Although William immediately refuted the story, the colonel and Mrs. Benét filled pages of vilification worse even than her attacks on Elinor. The colonel expressed his anger in a letter to Stephen:

> Kathleen cannot help lying and someday someone will repeat some of her remarks about Elinor to Elinor and the fat will be in the fire. Not but what they are true but they show up Kathleen for the damned hypocrite she is. William is under such obligations to them that he can hardly do anything no matter what they do or say. He wrote your mother they are to send him the money for his trip to California. I did not think a son of mine would do this. It is a great mortification though I ought to be used to it. . . . Norris is a bounder. . . . Neither he nor Kathleen has the least breeding or delicacy.[7]

Rosemary, who seldom criticized William, did understand why the Benéts were so upset: "It is such a difficult situation, for William has let them [the Norrises] take absolute care of the children for two years without raising a finger—yet I am sure Col. & Mrs. Benét feel his lack of responsibility keenly and long to have the children back in the family fold. Elinor doesn't encourage it." She asked her mother not to speak of the matter, "as it is the most intimate of family gossip but meanwhile the grandparents suffer." Her postscript softened her criticism: "How glad I am not to be under monetary obligations to anybody for my children! Poor William! Mine are all yours and mine!"

Mrs. Benét, long after William had denied the story, continued to attack Kay. "But why should Kathleen promulgate such a false story? Because she simply cannot tell the truth, for one thing." But in the same letter she revealed the great stress that she and the colonel must have been under, beyond the gossip: the destruction of their belongings in the recent fire, the moves from their spacious military quarters to boarding-houses in several cities, and, perhaps most of all, letting the children go to the other end of the country.

There was an added problem that even Stephen and Rosemary probably did not know about. Laura, whose one ambition was to have enough money to have the children with her sometimes, had become very ill after the children left. Mrs. Benét accused William of speaking flippantly about Laura:

> You should feel to your heart's core for your sister, who has been ig-nored & treated with contempt & impertinence, by those who are not worthy to brush her shoes—Yes, it was quite true about the river, though you speak of it as "seeking the briny"—and it is also true that she did not have a natural sleep for months and I discovered she was *taking a drug* & had a serious time & a most alarming time, getting it away from her. Ah, I tell you, I have been through some hell—[8]

Mrs. Benét left that month for Bedford Springs—an expensive cure, Rose-mary said, but probably psychologically good for her. Mrs. Benét thought that it ought to be done but followed that assertion with the comment to Stephen, "Ah, did you know that Leonard Bacon [a professor, writer, and family friend] had gone to Jung in Germany to be psychoanalyzed? Now if that is not the very limit!"[9]

William went to California to be with his children. On his way to the West Coast, he stopped to visit the Carrs. Stephen, who worried much about William, was glad to hear that Dr. Carr thought he looked well. Rosemary wrote, "I think he is amazingly young-looking, much more so than Laura, who is only a year older."

Stephen and Rosemary, free for the moment from family involvement, moved to Bizy, fifty miles from Paris in south Normandy. Their rented house at 48 rue de la Côte was very near the Myerses, and so the sum-mer promised beautiful surroundings and pleasant company. Stephen's Guggenheim grant had been renewed for six months, easing the financial problems for a time. On June 20 he wrote to John Farrar that *John Brown's Body* was three-quarters finished and should be ready in August. He gently declined Farrar's invitation to write a poem on Lindbergh. Farrar did publish Elinor's poem "Love to Stephen" in his *Bookman* that month.[10]

Rosemary was busy as typist of the final drafts of the poem, because retyping cost so much in Paris. The Philip Barrys had sent a charming invitation to visit them at their expense in Cannes again, but there were too many responsibilities with the new poem. Rosemary's support of Stephen's work, in addition to her responsibilities to so many people, was essential to his success. The nearest she came to a complaint was when she told her mother that "there ought to be a special prayer for authors' wives in the Episcopal service—they need and are expected to have the patience of Job." Years later, William Benét acknowledged her contribution to his brother's work in the essay "My Brother Stephen" in the *Saturday Review of Literature*. In the writing of *John Brown's Body*, he said, "it took the courage of his wife, too, of course—a courage and an admirable commonsense which she has never failed to show in an emergency."[11] But she had time to find much pleasure with the children. Pictures of Stephanie, now called Nini, show that she had grown to be a pretty girl, different from the first descriptions of her. She was learning her letters and had an excellent memory, and Thomas was a beautiful, laughing child who adored his sister.

At the end of August Stephen went to England for three days to visit William, who had just arrived after a visit to the children in California. Elinor sent Rosemary another elegant outfit and clothes from Poiret for the almost-year-old Tommy. As the typing of *John Brown's Body* was now complete, Rosemary wrote to Dr. Carr, "I think it is a great poem in spots, but being poetry will not make money. But if it is a satisfaction and pride to Stephen and a few people it will be worth it." She added that all his best stories recently were in *Country Gentleman*.[12]

Dr. Carr's situation was a source of worry for Rosemary that summer and fall. She sent some money to help with property taxes but could only commiserate as her mother described the difficulties of caring for Thomas Carr. "He made the days so unpleasant that I feared I would not be equal to the effort. . . . Dr. Campbell calls his attitude stubbornness & I am at a loss to name the condition that makes him deaf to every appeal."[13]

The social life of the Stephen Benéts resumed while the publishers in New York were reading Stephen's long poem. His friend John Carter paid a visit and brought his new bride, who educed Rosemary's occasional snobbishness: "She is a divorcée and English and a little ordinary and everyone wonders why on earth he married her."[14] Emily Kimbrough, an old friend and an executive with the *Ladies' Home Journal*, was more welcome. She wanted to make Richard Myers the Paris representative of the magazine, a move that would mean work for Rosemary. "If only I can collect some money together, I shall be of *some* use," she told her mother. Richard was of more immediate help, securing a job for her at *Town and Country* to write "Our Paris Letter," a column that allowed her to review the fashions and the cultural events of the great city. Her byline was prominently displayed every month. The first letter to her mother about the new position promised to send half her salary.

When they returned from their summer in Bizy, they settled in a small three-story house with a garden at 36 rue de Longchamp in Neuilly. Rosemary had time to read some memoirs and biographies. She found Margot Asquith's "absorbing" and listed Joseph Conrad, Boni de Castellane, Yvette Guilbert, and Frances Hodgson Burnett among her current choices. Burnett, she thought, was "a most silly sentimental person, the least interesting of them." She also found time to keep up to date on the political events of the time. She wrote to Dr. Carr:

> There has been a great feeling about Sacco & Vanzetti but I hope it will quiet down. Most people here say awful things about American justice without even knowing of what they were accused. I think they should not have kept them seven years, but now it is too hard for Gov. Fuller to act other than he has. The real issue has been obscured by so many things—it is no longer a single issue. It is funny though, our alternate popularity and unpopularity due to Lindberg [*sic*] or Sacco & Vanzetti.
>
> What do you think of Coolidge's decision not to run? Right, I think— Do you think Al Smith has a chance?[15]

Mrs. Benét devoted much of one letter to Stephen to the topic, but more in a gossipy mode: "The whole country is in an uproar about Sacco & Vanzetti—Lola Ridge & Ruth Hale went to Boston on the New York Committee. John dos Passos [*sic*] and Dorothy Parker were arrested at the Capitol." She reported that even well-dressed men and women were wearing black armbands, and Boston had been practically under martial law. "The few days [*sic*] reprieve has brought quiet again—but what next?" Her account of the demonstration was followed by the same question that

Rosemary had asked: "What did you think of Mr. Coolidge's decision not to run for a third term?"[16]

Kathleen Norris was in town with her sister Margaret (known as Mark), and Rosemary lunched with them. She wrote to apologize to her mother for Elinor's failure to call her when she was in Chicago to do a reading. Dr. Carr had heard the performance, but Rosemary was angry at Elinor's breach of the obligatory etiquette. Elinor had also failed to call on Aunt Margaret in Paris and was now going to be snubbed when the important Laurence Benéts arrived in New York.

Such petty matters did not occupy Rosemary for long. A cable arrived from Stephen's publisher that read, "Congratulations. Poem magnificent." That assessment was to change the fortunes of the Stephen Vincent Benét family. But there were still events that would intrude into the euphoria that followed. Stephanie had a tonsillectomy to improve a respiratory problem. Richard Myers sent a helpful message: "I know she will be alright 1st because she is husky—2nd because Doumenge is a wizard & 3rd because with children her age it isn't a grave affaire [sic]. And if it is necessary—it ought to done—otherwise she may always have colds & bronchitis, etc." That proved not to be a lasting problem, but then Stephen had news about Laura—ill and in the hospital. Rosemary said that Mrs. Benét was wild with anxiety and thought that Laura had just escaped death. Connie Guion, the doctor who served so many of the family, found double vision, partial paralysis of muscles of the eye, and engorgement of blood vessels in the brain. The patient, she said, was at times irrational and should be watched. As Rosemary told her mother, this was such hard luck for everybody, especially just before the holidays.

Nevertheless, two lovely Christmas poems—one from Rosemary to Stephen and another from Stephen to Rosemary—testify to the love and the strength of hope that the couple still maintained.

Rosemary's poem, "To Stephen, Christmas—1927—Paris," read:

Frankincense and myrrh, I want
I must do with Houbigant—
Silks of richest hues and dyes
I shall have to sham with ties—
Books I covet for your sake,
Here's one small book by Mr. Blake—
Angels, children, light and wine

Which might make your eyes ashine
Come reduced as silly toys—
May they bring you Christmas joy
But the love that comes with these
Is as deep as deepest seas.

Stephen's poem, "Merry Christmas—1927!" accompanied a pair of crystal
candlesticks:

These candles are alike, yet they are two.
Take one for the body's worth
Which is more beautiful than rain or spring,
A little body made of sun and earth,
Some flowers (the whitest, these), a cloud, a feather
The talk of certain birds and certain streams,
The silence of proud dreams,
All living in peace, all held in peace together
By the bright silver penny of the heart
You found long since within a fairy-ring—
Take this candle—not because its art
Can light a path for you along the night
But rather for your hand to give it light—
But stay a moment ere you do depart,
The candle sticks are two
There is another You,
No flesh, however fair,
Can bind that fire and air
Nor any night inherit
That luster, that intense
Thing beyond excellence
And all the tricks of time—
So, from your lover, who has made much rhyme
But found few proud enough to match your name
Or your deep steadfastness,
Accept this second tot of glass and flame
And in its crystal read your crystal spirit
And in the flame the love he cherishes.

CHAPTER 10

Pain and Grief

The beginning of 1928 found Stephen ill. Dr. Carr prescribed mineral spirits, including very detailed instructions about dosage, for his severe stomach pains. A new problem was diagnosed as Vincent's angina, or trench mouth, a disease common in those whose resistance is weak. His mother and Rosemary both worried because he was so thin. "It seems to be a hard year for the Benét health—or maybe last year was the hard one and now it will improve," Rosemary told her mother. Although Laura seemed to be recuperating at home with her parents in Westtown at the first of the year and was looking forward to assuming new duties as the associate editor of the *New York Evening Post,* two weeks later a new siege was diagnosed as encephalitis. Many doctors were involved, three of them distinguished specialists. Thomas Carr's condition continued to deteriorate and to frustrate his physician wife. And in New York Elinor was recovering from a bout with ptomaine.

Kay and Cigi, who traveled to France often, were visiting Rosemary and Stephen en route. Kay was distressed because Mrs. Benét, resentful that the Norrises were caring for William's children, had written a "dreadful" letter. But the children were more charming and intelligent than ever, according to Kay's "eloquent" report. Rosemary's letter expressed her continuing unqualified admiration of Kathleen Norris.

On a happier note, John Farrar said that *John Brown's Body* was one of the most remarkable manuscripts ever to come into the publishing office. Stephen, of course, was very pleased. He wasn't sure about the "genius" that Farrar had proclaimed, but it did take persistence, he admitted. At this time it was agreed that the book would not be released until fall. Stephen wrote to his old college friend Phelps Putnam that he would be in France until then; he could live more cheaply in France. "I'm not going back to go crazy in New York again," he added. His attitude toward that city is expressed in his last novel, *James Shore's Daughter:* "There was nothing like it in the world. It was beyond vulgarity, for it was beyond belief. All other cities I had known had been places where people could live. But this was not a place where people could live—it was a triumphal shaft, pointed angrily at the sky and always rising—a shaft upon which the hard electric beam wrote inscriptions too swiftly for the eye."[1] William, however, remembered something different when he wrote to Stephen in February that there were no parties as there were in the old times when he and Steve with Rosemary and Elinor gathered at Marta's.

In March Farrar and company agreed to an earlier release for *John Brown's Body* and asked Stephen to come to New York for the event. Stephen's objections were several: his Guggenheim grant had run out and he could not afford the trip, even though they offered to pay for his passage; he had been sicker than he thought and was behind in his work; he did not think his physical presence in America would mean much to the success of the book because it was the interesting thing about him, and besides, he had lived in New York long enough for people to know him. Two weeks later, however, he wrote hastily to say that he had just heard of his father's death. He asked Farrar to send the check for the advance on his poem to William, who would be in charge of arrangements at home. Stephen told Farrar that his father had understood him completely: "He was the best man I ever knew or am likely to know."[2] As Rosemary told her mother, "You can imagine what a shock this is to Stephen who adored his father beyond anything in the world."

Colonel Benét had died of angina pectoris, suffering two attacks a week apart. He had appeared to improve between them and then died suddenly. His widow made arrangements for a large military funeral with burial at Arlington National Cemetery. Everyone had assumed that he was the strongest of the family, and his loss would be very difficult for Mrs. Benét, whose responsibilities included Laura, still sick at home, and Aunt Agnes, now totally helpless. Furthermore, the military pension on which they depended would now stop. But both William and Stephen were very generous, according to Mrs. Benét, and with Elinor in England, William spent his weekends at Westtown, Pennsylvania, to help as much as possible.

In Paris the spring was devoted to correcting galleys of *John Brown's*

Body and other publishing matters. When the Book of the Month committee made the poem its August selection, in large part because of John Farrar's promotion, Stephen was thrilled and incredulous at the printing of sixty-five thousand copies. He wrote to Farrar, "I really did not expect such a thing, in my usual sour way, and was most pleasurably taken aback. That is swell."[3] He had decided that the dedication of the work would be "To my mother and the memory of my father."

By June Rosemary was concerned enough about her mother that she suggested a vacation as a respite from her father's increasingly demanding care. Dr. Carr regretted that she could not leave: "To go away is not practical for reasons too intimate & lengthy to write in full. Father has become a neurasthenic, who must be disciplined for his sake and mine."[4]

But both Stephen and Rosemary were sick themselves that month and decided to go to Cabourg, northwest of Paris in Calvados, where their intended rest was interrupted by the news of two members of their extended family. Elinor, while visiting friends near Henley, fell down a flight of stairs, seriously injuring her back. As she described the incident to Nancy, she had suddenly lost consciousness; the accident was probably the first of three strokes that would cause her death in another few months. Her hosts, not realizing the extent of her injuries, put her on a train back to London, where her maid cared for her. Her distress was heightened by the American press printing news of her having jumped through a window to her death, to which she responded with a poem, never published, "To the Gentlemen of the Press," which ended with the couplet "And, if you have backbones to break, / God mend them straight as mine is." Mrs. Benét conveyed her sense of slight scandal by her usual device of asking a question: "What *did* you think of Elinor's accident?"

The second Hoyt adventure that summer was widely reported in the press, as well, with about the same degree of accuracy. In July Elinor's younger brother Morton, on a ship returning from France, jumped overboard—according to various reports, because he was settling an argument about his chances of being rescued, or because he was despondent about yet another separation from his wife, Jeanne, or because he was trying impress a debutante onboard, or just because he was drunk. He spent the remainder of the crossing in the brig. The *Herald Tribune* revived the story in December when the couple married for the third time in the Little Church around the Corner. The news report credited the July plunge for the reconciliation. As Rosemary wrote, "But what a family!"

From the Villa Soleil in Cabourg, Stephen wrote to Farrar about the reviews of *John Brown's Body*, mostly favorable, and the kind letters that had been sent from the United States. He agreed to go to New York when Farrar sent a welcome check. "Never did I think that I would return to New York with any money left after tipping the library-steward. But it will be a very pleasant—and novel—sensation."[5] He arranged to sail aboard the *Île-de-France* on August 8 for interviews and some speaking engagements.

Stephen met his mother and Laura in New York, staying at the Hotel Marquis for a week. He thought that they were over their initial shock at the colonel's death, but he recognized how hard the loss was for them. Part of his time was spent in finding a residence where they could find some comfort and stability. After time with his family he planned to go to Chicago to see the Carrs in September. Rosemary stayed behind, as she had during his trips to Cannes and England, to meet deadlines for her twice-monthly column for *Town and Country* and to care for the children.

She heard from William, who had arrived in England to be with Elinor, that his mother was well and courageous, but he added that Laura was very nervous and upset—that she was not a mature person. Rosemary tried to put the best face on the comment: "He meant mature in the sense of experienced—rich in life."[6]

William had a more personal shock when he learned during his brief visit that Elinor had fallen in love with Clifford Woodhouse, an Englishman who had been her host at Henley. William's autobiographical poem, using fictional names for Clifford and Elinor, describes the moment when he became aware of the relationship:

> His own eyes
> witnessed a gaze not meant for any other
> that for an interval seemed to transfix
> Alan and Sylvia   the instant was
> suspended in golden light.[7]

From that time, the marriage of William Rose Benét and Elinor Wylie became more complex than ever and a greater problem for those about them. Rosemary became the family's intermediary even for small matters, as when she learned from Richard Myers that the Poiret establishment, the source of her lovely gifts of couture clothes from Elinor, had not been paid for them. In a postscript to his letter of August 31, Myers wrote: "Mme

Helene seems to be worried about Elinor's bill chez Poiret. I told her to telephone you for her London address. Wouldn't you know she'd do that?"

When Stephen returned, Rosemary was able to send her mother some money from her *Town and Country* salary and from Stephen's new earnings. She praised her husband, saying he was "kind, loyal, full of courage and modesty." They were beset by visitors, she said, among them the writer Leonard Bacon, who was a good friend of all the Benéts. But at least they now had two servants to help with care of the children and household chores.

November found most of the family in their sickbeds with what was diagnosed as the grippe, and in Stephanie's case a further development of bronchitis. Rosemary's concern was that all the barking with coughs would disturb Stephen. Her own cough prevented her from attending *Manon* at the Opéra Comique, and she sent Stephen in her place. "We always seem to spend Thanksgiving in some sort of a flurry of sickness," she complained to her mother. The family gossip was about Elinor and William; Rosemary thought that Elinor had found that England was her spiritual home and therefore kept deferring her trip back to New York; William maintained an expensive apartment in New York, hoping that she would soon return. She had not written to Stephen and Rosemary for some time and had not mentioned a word about Stephen's new book. Mrs. Benét wrote to Stephen that William was "playing around with some pretty ones" and she was glad that he was having fun. Rosemary confessed that they heard all sorts of rumors but did not know just what was happening.

Mrs. Benét, although she had written a vitriolic letter to Kathleen, met the Norrises when they were in New York. She sent her gossip to Rosemary: Kay was tremendously made up; Kay's sister Mark had blondined her hair, which gave it a startling yellow color; and Charles thought that his publishers had not been promoting his latest book, *The Foolish Virgin*, as they should. "Mon Dieu!" Mrs. Benét added.

The Stephen Benéts' literary successes afforded new social as well as financial opportunities. In December they lunched with some of the Roosevelt family—Theodore Jr., Kermit, and their wives, along with four other people. "They were most cordial to us and are very pleasant hearty people," Rosemary told her mother.[8]

Stephen wrote to Laura congratulating her on a story published in the *Forum*. He encouraged her often, telling her that nothing would bring success in publishing like publishing, and he provided her with a more comfortable place to write, moving her and Mrs. Benét from their dismal rooms into the Judson Hotel in Washington Square, where they were also able to enjoy concerts and plays. He also sent a check to Lola Ridge, another writer frequently in need of the financial help that the Benét family so often provided.

After changing her sailing date for the fifth time, Elinor docked in New York on the eleventh and spent a few frantic days seeing friends and family, reading her new sonnet sequence, "One Person," to everyone. On Sunday, December 16, she arranged those sonnets and the other poems of *Angels and Earthly Creatures* for publication and suddenly died after another stroke. When Rosemary and Stephen learned of her death by reading the newspaper account, Stephen thought that it was because William was too grief stricken to tell them. The fact was that Mrs. Benét had decided to lessen the shock by having Richard Myers tell them, but her cable was delayed because she sent it to an old address. Rosemary wrote to her mother that her own judgment about Elinor had been wrong; she was not angry, but ill. To William she wrote, "There was no one like her—that mixture of brilliance, sensitiveness and courage will not come again. . . . I shall miss her with all my heart."[9]

Mrs. Benét's letters described the family's grieving, especially during a Christmas Eve visit to William's apartment, where he had created a shrine to Elinor. After donating Elinor's Shelley papers to the British Museum, he gave the rest of her estate to her son, Philip Hichborn. An impressive memorial service, with poets Padraic Colum and Robert Nathan as speakers, was held at St. Mark's. A snowstorm and high winds prevented Mrs. Benét and Laura from attending.

Many friends sent condolences to Stephen and Rosemary, as well as to William. Edna St. Vincent Millay, who had placed a wreath of laurel on the head of her dead friend, said that for her the loss of Elinor was so great that she wondered how people could bear such things.[10] Douglas Moore, who also had attended the funeral, gave a full description of it and added an elegant tribute to a poet whom he admired: "Losing Elinor seems like a dimming process of the whole of existence. She never seemed exactly like a person—rather some unearthly creature that was misplaced on the earth but was often very nice about it. I loved her very much and I shall always miss her. As for Bill . . . his nobility and kindness were things so great as to raise the whole level of human achievement in character."[11] Mrs. Benét agreed with Marianne Moore, who said that Elinor had finished her best work, and added her own conclusion: "She would never have lived on, a cripple & disfigured by a partial paralysis. She would have taken her life, I am sure."[12] Dr. Carr, recognizing the connection among all the families surrounding Elinor, agreed: "It seems death is sometimes very kind. There was a possibility of invalidism & great incapacity in Elinor's condition. She would suffer greatly under either affliction & her friends would share equally her distress. My experience the last six years would not permit me to choose this fate for her or for those who loved her."[13]

The holiday season that year remained difficult for all the families, but Stephen and Rosemary made the best of Christmas by spending the day with Richard and Alice Lee Myers. In spite of Stephen's remarkable successes, 1928 had brought, in Mrs. Benét's words, "pain and grief enough to a last a life time."

CHAPTER 11

From Paris to New York

"Dearest Mother," Rosemary wrote, "New Year's day is always a great festival in Paris even more so than Christmas. People make family calls; the servants all expect tips—there are presents and dinners and gaiety. We spent it quietly—not wishing to celebrate because of Elinor." Rosemary worked on her Paris report for *Town and Country* and then took the children to visit Laurence and Margaret Benét, where they made her extremely proud, although she had to admit that such behavior was not usual. Stephen received a cable from his family that day telling him that all was well and that William's son, Jim, had arrived from California for a visit that would be a great comfort.

Mrs. Benét wrote a fifteen-page letter to Rosemary a week later with news significant and trivial. She thanked her for a Christmas gift—a cloth and napkins that would allow her to have guests for tea in her room. She explained that she had had only two visitors so far at the Judson Hotel— Lola Ridge and E. B. Dewing, a woman writer who criticized her choice of tea. Several pages of her letter were devoted to possible places for Stephen's family to live when they returned to the United States. She telephoned Richard Myers, who was in Philadelphia at the time, to ask him to look for a place there. She scouted the neighborhoods in Philadelphia, on which she had very strong opinions, including one that she found unacceptable: it was too far from the town center, and the cars were full of Negroes and Italians, she said, echoing the typical xenophobic and racist attitudes of the twenties. Germantown or Chestnut Hill would be more suitable, and Germantown had a Montessori school that was perfect for Stephanie. Furthermore, she knew a Main Line woman who was sailing on the *Île-de-France* soon and could be of advantage in placing the family in the right society in Philadelphia if Rosemary would invite her to dinner. As Mrs. Benét no longer had her own household to control, she gladly took more and more responsibility for directing Stephen and Rosemary's.

Rosemary expressed her impatience at her mother-in-law's interference a few years later:

> Mrs. Benét is so nervous and spoiled. There is another tragedy, when you think of Laura's life! She is a selfish mother—constantly wanting to absorb and interfere with her children—just can't leave them alone. Thank goodness the boys have not fallen under her domination completely—But she is strong-willed and spoiled—and I tell you I have to watch my step! It is smother-love—not mother love!
>
> If only she had done some work in her life! She has nothing to turn her mind to. I am so grateful that you brought me up to think work important and to know its value.[1]

Rosemary's satisfaction in the success that her writing brought kept away the depression that she had confessed only to Catharine. And she was fortunate that her opportunities to publish her work came more frequently as her literary reputation increased.

Social life in Paris was busy with old friends as well as American visitors. Aunt Margaret invited them to dinner with the young Adlai Stevensons of Bloomington and Chicago, long before the grandson of Grover Cleveland's vice president himself became governor of Illinois, UN ambassador, and presidential candidate. Rosemary and Stephen lunched with Edna St. Vincent Millay and "her equally delightful husband," Eugen Boissevain. DuBose Heyward, author of *Porgy* and fellow MacDowell colonist, visited, and a Miss Hoyt, one of Elinor's aunts—"a very nice person"—came to call.

Domestic problems with the servants bothered both Rosemary and her mother. In Paris there were "great ructions" with Françoise, who had made a scene, snatching Tommy from her arms and slapping Stephanie. Rosemary thought, however, that she would keep the maid, excusing her temper on the grounds that it came with red hair and an inordinate fondness for Tommy. But Françoise was spoiling him and scolding Stephanie constantly. In Chicago Dr. Carr dismissed her maid, Nellie, who, according to her account, had been dishonest and disloyal, making the care of Thomas Carr an even greater problem.

Plans for return to the United States were begun early in May. John Farrar offered his apartment when they arrived in New York, and Leonard Bacon offered his house in Peace Dale, Rhode Island, for a year. May was a banner month for Stephen when he was awarded the Pulitzer Prize for poetry. The cable announcing the award came during a dinner party, and because the guests were on a diet, Rosemary and Stephen waited until later to toast the good news. Just after that they went to Cannes to visit Philip and Ellen Barry. Their villa, Stephen wrote to William, was a demiparadise. "We led a gay life, swimming, talking, going around in large cars and drinking at appropriate intervals. You would like those people and I hope to see a lot of them when they get back to America." Other special people who were everyone's favorites were the Childs. Charles Child, brother of Paul and brother-in-law of Julia, had just painted an enchanting portrait of Rosemary that was greatly admired in Paris.

The remainder of that summer was difficult. A visitor reported that the Neuilly house was all torn up, with boxes everywhere. They were not taking much furniture, but the books, the children's things, and the dog that had followed them home from the park made packing a chore. Rosemary was training someone to take over "Our Paris Letter" in *Town and Country*. In spite of the chaos, both Stephen and Rosemary were gracious to a young woman, Caroline Lovett, whose only connection with them was a drawing class with Stephen fifteen years before in Augusta. Miss Lovett's letter to her mother about the visit reveals that she is the kind of woman who Mrs. Benét thought would help their assimilation into Philadelphia society; she suggested Rosemont, Bryn Mawr, and some places on the Main Line as desirable. She also very precisely described Rosemary as lovely at thirty-one: "Her skin is soft and white with not much cheek color. Her eyes are a blue grey, one a wee bit larger than the other. Her nose is aquiline and her upper lip very long. Her chin is more inclined to recede than protrude, a rather retiring little chin—a very expressive mouth. Her manner was charming and cordial and very easy."[2]

The news from the families was distressing, ranging from annoyance to serious matters. Mrs. Benét wrote that Laura was unhappy at a writer's colony in Saratoga Springs. Yaddo, she said, was very beautiful, but too sophisticated for her, and "there's a group of young Jews there now, not wildly interesting for her."[3] A greater problem was that Aunt Agnes had to be placed in an institution. Also serious was William's problem with

Elinor's final interment alongside the Hoyt family at Forty Fort Cemetery in Pennsylvania. At the last minute no members of her family took responsibility, and he had to travel with her body to Pennsylvania. The gravestone that had been selected gave the wrong date of birth and the name Elinor Wylie (Elinor Morton Hoyt). There was no mention of either the Hichborn or Benét name. "It is perfectly ghastly," his mother told Stephen. "If you had only been here!" But he would later have the difficult assignment to fly to England to put Elinor's complicated affairs in order. At the same time Rosemary worried about her mother, whose health was poor, but who had assured her that she could not help: "My beloved Rosemary, do not regret your inability to be near us. You could not have changed the situation in the least. I am a trained nurse, a capable one, & a physician, Dr. Campbell is a good doctor & a friend & we have failed."[4] Rosemary advised her mother to put Thomas Carr in a hospital and offered to help with expenses.

The sail to New York on the *Île-de-France* on August 13 did not go well. Rosemary had hoped that the first-class privileges that Richard had tried to arrange and the help of a maid, Corantine, would mean a pleasant passage. She had brought some evening gowns "in hopes of grandeur." But their accommodations were not those they had signed for, and their treatment by the crew was not acceptable. She wrote to Richard Myers about the behavior of the French Line, and his reply was: "They'll pay for it!" His letter of August 29 to "Dearest old Benéts" began, "My fury knows no bounds! The duplicity of the French Line makes me feel that never again will I travel on it nor allow anybody I know to travel on it." But even his fury found release in his musical talent; he insisted that he and Stephen collaborate on a song about "Corantine thru Quarantine."

On arrival in New York the family moved into John Farrar's apartment briefly, as originally planned, then to Douglas Moore's house until September. The move into their own apartment was delayed because the painting was not finished, and they had to live for a while in a hotel. Finally they relocated for the fifth time in five weeks to what Stephen called a "quaint little walk-up" at 60 Ninety-third Street. There were compensating advantages; it was near the park and just around the corner from several friends—Stanley Rinehart, John Farrar, and Ethel Andrews. The invitation to stay in Leonard Bacon's beautiful house would be accepted some years later. Almost as soon as they were settled in their apartment, they made a trip to Chicago to help Dr. Carr move from her Hyde Park address to a small apartment on Dorchester Street. She asked Rosemary not to bring the children because of Thomas Carr's deterioration. Stephen helped at the Carr residence but had time for a speech at the University of Chicago and tea with President Robert Hutchins and his wife.

While Rosemary and Stephen were in Chicago, Mrs. Benét cared for the children and saw to their religious education. After hearing "Our Father which art in heaven," three-year-old Tommy interrupted, "But Papa is in Chicago." Stephanie, two years older and more sophisticated, instructed her father in the vice of gluttony and explained the concept of the Holy Ghost to him. Stephen confessed to William, "I find religious instruction for the Young very hard."

Stephen and Rosemary were now in their new residence, close to the schools that they had chosen for the children and to the family members who were more in need of their attention than ever. But the problem of financial security, after only a few months of respite, began to plague them again. Stephen's windfall from *John Brown's Body* and the works that immediately followed, as well as Rosemary's modest salary from her contributions to magazines, had been invested in what Stephen called "good, sound, New Era stocks." But just as they returned to live in the United States, the market collapsed, and few investors escaped financial disaster. As so often before, Stephen was forced to consider the most immediate route to supporting his family. At Thanksgiving Rosemary told her mother that he had been invited by D. W. Griffith to go to Hollywood to write a film about Lincoln that would star Walter Huston in the title role.

On December 2 he left for Hollywood and the United Artists studio. The commitment meant that the family would be separated at Christmas during their first year away from their familiar surroundings in France. Griffith treated Stephen well, but the internecine politics of Hollywood were almost intolerable. "Nowhere have I seen such shining waste, stupidity and conceit as in the business and managing end of this industry. Whoopee!" Stephen wrote to Carl Brandt. The consolation for all this annoyance was the handsome salary that allowed the studios to entice such writers as Dorothy Parker, F. Scott Fitzgerald, Thornton Wilder, and William Faulkner. Most writers, however, agreed with the playwright Sidney Howard, who walked into Stephen's office one day, sat down, and said, "God, how I hate this place." Stephen's goal was clear, as he told

Rosemary: "We're going to get a nice house out of this—concentrate on the house—I am." One postscript said that she would get sapphires, too. He worked furiously, both on his own writing and in the conferences with others. He did have one Sunday free to drive the 450 miles to Palo Alto to see the Norrises and William's children, who he reported looked fine and were perfectly charming. Everyone was looking forward to being with the Benét family for Christmas. In Stephen's final days at the movie studio an article sent to *Variety* claiming that the producer had changed Stephen's script drove him to threaten to sue. The matter was resolved with a published apology. On February 8 he completed his assignment on the four versions of the Abraham Lincoln film and was on his way to meet Rosemary in Chicago.

Rosemary told the Myerses that Stephen had not succumbed to Hollywood's invitations until they offered him a vast sum that he could not refuse. He had met Lillian Gish, who was his dream girl, and almost went dancing with Delores del Rio. It was just like Stephen, she told them, to say, "Thank Heaven the party fell through." She teased Richard and Alice Lee, "What's this I hear about you & the Scott Fitzgeralds getting so intimate? Assure me instantly that we are your favorite literary couple."[5] Richard's reply was: "Of course, you are our favorite literary couple. You don't suppose the Fitzgeralds could supplant you in our esteem? My gawd! I now try to find excuses for dodging them. They may be nice but they're not our style. And too damn fatiguing with their heavy drinking." Scott, he said, could finish much more work if he did not finish so many bottles of Scotch. Richard complained about the people who were about when it was always the Stephen Benéts they wanted to see.

Rosemary, Stephanie, and Tommy, along with the maid Corantine, spent the holidays in Richmond, Virginia, with the McVeys—her Aunt Jo, Uncle Harry, and Cousin Margaret. Dr. Carr arrived to be with them for a few days but left the day after Christmas and seemed to be too tired even to enjoy the children. Her mother's state of mind made Rosemary's own depression worse, and she resolved to get more rest, along with the medication that Dr. Guion had prescribed. But she was enjoying the visit and declared that both Richmond and Philadelphia had a dignity that could not be found in New York. They would leave Virginia soon, however, to meet Kathleen Norris and the cousins before they left for California.

Right: Rosemary's parents, Dr. Rachel Hickey Carr and Thomas Carr, c. 1910. Courtesy of Thomas Carr Benét.

Left: Rosemary at age two or three. Courtesy of Thomas Carr Benét.

Left: Stephen Vincent Benét, 1921. Yale Collection of American Literature, Beinecke Rare Book and Manuscript Library.

Below: A costume party with Paris friends and family, February 1921. Bottom row from left: Douglas Moore, Rosemary, Mrs. Barney, Catharine Hopkins, Emily Moore, Margaret Cox Benét, Alice Lee Myers, Lucia Page. Top row from left: Stephen, Quincy Porter, Colin Mackall, Leon Stolz (city editor of the *Tribune*), Richard Myers, Laurence Benét, Henry Carter, Stanley Hawks, Danford Barney. Courtesy of Thomas Carr Benét.

Rosemary in Paris, 1922. Yale Collection of American Literature, Beinecke Rare Book and Manuscript Library.

Above: Stephen and
Rosemary in Paris,
1922. Yale Collection
of American Literature,
Beinecke Rare Book and
Manuscript Library.

Right: Rosemary Carr
and Richard Myers in
Paris, 1922. Yale Collec-
tion of American Lit-
erature, Beinecke Rare
Book and Manuscript
Library.

Richard Myers and Stephen Vincent Benét in Paris, 1922. Yale Collection of American Literature, Beinecke Rare Book and Manuscript Library.

Left: Dr. Rachel Hickey Carr and Stephanie, 1925. Yale Collection of American Literature, Beinecke Rare Book and Manuscript Library.

Right: The Benéts' Christmas card, 1924. Courtesy of Thomas Carr Benét.

Stephen, Rosemary, and Stephanie, 1926. Yale Collection of American Literature, Beinecke Rare Book and Manuscript Library.

Above left: Rosemary and Stephanie in their garden, 1929. Courtesy of Thomas Carr Benét.

Above right: Rosemary, Stephanie, and Thomas, 1928. Courtesy of Thomas Carr Benét.

Right, clockwise: Stephen, Rosemary, Stephanie, and Thomas, 1927. Courtesy of Thomas Carr Benét.

CHAPTER 12

End of a Decade

On New Year's Day Rosemary wrote to Stephen, still in California, "You have been gone four weeks and three days! May the rest not seem so long! I shall count the days. . . . This visit has been grand because I have been a little less lonely than in New York. I am so fond of all my Richmond relatives and they lead a gay cheerful life which Heaven knows I need at this time." Her reports on the children were also positive. Stephanie was learning more English and even making New Year's resolutions. Both children enjoyed both the company and the food in Richmond. As for Rosemary, the luxury of late sleep in the mornings helped to lighten her depression. But if Steve had any more liaisons with the movies, she promised, they would all go to California.

When Rosemary returned to New York she wrote again to Richard and Alice Lee. The holiday seasons, she lamented, are full of "alarums and excursions." The last day in Richmond she had a call that her father was gravely ill. She left the children and Corantine, who spoke no English, at a hotel near Mrs. Benét. Her father had improved when she arrived. There were happier moments in New York, as she saw the Barrys and the MacLeishes frequently. She still thought much about the Paris scene that she had once written about: "How are the new fashions? I miss the opening along with a lot of other things."[1]

When she finally met Stephen, he was ill, forced by arthritis to use a cane and further plagued by a variety of illnesses that had been present to one degree or another for several years. In the next months he wrote little and had to decline invitations to speak. In addition to caring for him, Rosemary responded to messages from her mother about Thomas Carr's condition. One letter said, "Father is a great care, in fact as much of a burden as he can make of himself & without the least spirit of co-operation. . . . The killing thing is the necessity of being ever on the alert with him & his heartless taking advantage of me when I am serving him."[2] Now as she sent a message that the end was near, her comment changed: "He has been a wonderful patient in his stoical acceptance of his disabilities & in his total absence of any complaint & in his confidence in my efforts to care for him." But she added, "You and Stephen have made possible my holding out to the end."[3] Thomas Carr died on March 21, and after a visit to her mother, Rosemary reassured her that she had done everything possible.

To recover from their trauma, the Benéts rented a house from their friend Pierre Hazard in Peace Dale, Rhode Island, where they stayed until November. But the spring and summer of 1930 marked the end of much of the hope, high spirits, and romance that had begun just a decade before in Paris. Both Rosemary's and Stephen's beloved fathers were dead, and their mothers were inconsolable. Laura's condition, both physical and mental, was fragile, at times even perilous. Elinor Wylie's sudden death had left William Benét bereft after a devastating ending to their marriage. Catharine Hopkins, Rosemary's only confidante and sustaining spirit, had died at thirty-three under difficult medical and moral circumstances. And now Stephen's health was so distressful that he could write little and lecture not at all for many months. It would never allow him to be without discomfort for the remaining few years of his life. Fortunately for him, the children, and the other survivors, there was Rosemary.

CHAPTER 13

Good-Byes

In March 1943 Rosemary Carr Benét began a long letter to her husband, Stephen. It was written in the blank space where he had just left off the entries in his diary at the time of his death, as though, by recording her feelings and the events of the day, she could keep his spirit alive.

> My dearest love, twenty-two years ago today we were engaged. Then my life,—my real life began. Now it is ended. I remember you wrote me the next day in Paris saying it was St. Patrick's day. This is the first time, I think that we have even been separated on that day. I do not believe that we ever were apart on a wedding anniversary either, in those years from 1921 to now. This is the first time you have not sent me flowers on the 17th.
>
> This has been the most agonizing horrible time of my life. I cannot tell you of the bitterness. One does not die of grief, I know that now. I hope it does not seem silly to you for me to be writing all this down. But I have had the habit so long to turn to you with everything, to talk things over, to report the small happenings as well as the big ones that I cannot break it now. I should die, if I didn't. (That is not true, for I know now that I am made of iron and reinforced concrete not to have died already) . . [.] but I should explode. I am going to put things down, little by little. Oh my darling, where are you? I feel so hopelessly lost without you. It is an ache and an agony, not just missing.

As a poet herself, Rosemary understood the consolation that words could provide as she recounted her current experiences with their family and friends, quoted his lines that comforted her, and expressed her grief often.

She talked about small changes brought about during wartime: there were to be no Fifth Avenue buses on Sundays, which meant they would stay at home. She asked his advice about the problems that now faced her: "What did you really mean to do with your diary?" Although John Farrar, his editor, thought it should be kept, she remembered that Stephen had once told her to burn it, that it was too frank for preservation; he had noted even the times that they made love ("delightful with J at 2 A.M.!"). And she made promises to him: "I feel that my life now is a *dedicated* one, To preserve your manuscripts and all the precious souvenirs of your life . . . and to bring up the children." (With the birth of Rachel in 1931, there were now three.)

Rosemary described a recurrent dream that had bothered her even when Stephen was living:

Now comes the nightmare,
—The retrospect that shakes all true lovers
—That I might not have met you
I might not have taken the train OR the boat
I might since I love to waltz
Have married a dancing boy
I might have stayed on to study
   OR had a cold and a fever
   And lost you forever—
OR wanted to go home or to Rome
Instead of to France—
I might have lost you forever—[1]

She continued to write in the months following ("Grief is an agony." "Like the moon I only shone with the reflected light from the sun." "So in the end all lessons came from him—love, birth & death."). She expressed her despair not only in her words but also in her very person for years. Almost a decade later, one friend described her as "a pale, shadowy social presence, the Victorian widow who has never recovered from her grief." But she added that it would be worth digging for the "witty, perceptive, acute mind." To know her would be to find her "shrewd taste and lovely humor," and "a spine of iron under the willowy white flesh."[2]

In 1977 Rosemary's younger daughter, Rachel, noted with less generosity her memories of growing up in a mourning household: "I had been raised in a home that revolved around my father, a gifted and endearing man. My mother adored him, friends flocked to him; whatever he did or said seemed to have a special grace. He died when I was 11, leaving me to flounder through six miserable years with my lonely and grieving mother."[3] Rachel, who, like Stephen, won literary prizes before graduation from high school and was once proclaimed an even better writer than her father, disdained the family profession and chose to study anthropology instead. On February 16, 1990, the *Boston Globe* published an obituary noting her work as a counselor at several rehabilitation centers, especially Rosie's Place, Hope House, and WomanPlace in Cambridge.

The other children, away at school during these years, escaped Rachel's despondency; Stephanie was at the Brearley School and then went on to Swarthmore and the Columbia School of Nursing. She died in 2005, survived by eight children and six grandchildren. Thomas attended Philips Exeter Academy and Yale University. After his years in the Field Service and the Army he became an outstanding journalist, serving as the longtime editorial page editor of the *Chronicle* in San Francisco, where he now lives.

The older members of the immediate family who survived the 1920s were Rosemary's and Stephen's mothers and Stephen's brother and sister. Frances Benét died in 1940, and Dr. Carr in 1946 after having financial and health problems. William Rose Benét married twice more after Elinor Wylie's death. His professional career prospered; in 1941 he was awarded the Pulitzer Prize for his autobiography in verse, *The Dust Which Is God*, and his *Reader's Encyclopedias* are standard references, both in the American and world literature editions.

After 1940 Laura Benét, too, began a remarkable literary productivity, writing biographies of Poe, Shelley, Coleridge, Thackeray, Washington Irving, Emily Dickinson, and Jenny Lind for young readers, along with poetry, fiction, and a memoir, *When William Rose, Stephen Vincent and I Were Young*. When she died in 1979, surviving all the other members of her immediate family, she was buried alongside her parents in Arlington National Cemetery.

Part of the reason for Rosemary's great desolation after the death of Stephen Vincent Benét was the contrast between her present loneliness and the exhilaration of their early years together. The excitement of the 1920s in Paris and New York and the presence of many interesting and talented friends were the ingredients for a glamorous and memorable period in her life. But even without France and Stephen, those friends—Douglas and Emily Moore, Richard and Alice Lee Myers, John Farrar, Philip and Ellen Barry—remained steadfast in their devotion to her and to Stephen's memory.

After the Paris years the Moores lived in New York, where Douglas was a member of the faculty at Columbia University until his retirement in 1962. He composed many orchestral works and several operas, including *The Ballad of Baby Doe* and *The Devil and Daniel Webster,* based on Benét's short story. Rosemary visited the Moores often at their home on Long Island. Douglas Moore died in 1969.

Richard and Alice Lee Myers remained in Paris until 1932, when he joined the Lehmann Corporation, a wine and liquor company. He composed music for plays by Yale friends Archibald MacLeish and Philip Barry and was also an associate editor of *Gourmet* and a contributor to *Town and Country.* After a long illness he died in 1958.

Philip and Ellen Barry continued to invite Rosemary for visits after Philip became one of American's most prominent playwrights. His successes included *Paris Bound* and *The Philadelphia Story.* In East Hampton a few months before Stephen's death, Barry proposed an epitaph that Benét liked: "Even Stephen? *He* must go? Even Stephen? Even so." Barry survived Benét by only six years.

John Farrar remained close to Rosemary and a supporter of her work long after his early encouragement in publishing and his strong moral support in the Benét political ventures of the thirties and early forties. He edited the *Bookman,* founded the publishing house of Farrar and Rinehart, and later created Farrar, Straus and Giroux. He died in 1974.

Kathleen Norris lovingly cared for the children of William Rose Benét, even as she maintained her furious pace of writing novels, magazine articles, and political columns. During the thirties she took an active part in movements for pacifism and women's rights, only one reason that Rosemary continued to find much to admire about her. Charles, also an author, although less prolific and less talented, died in 1945, twenty-one years before Kathleen.

All these people and many others, famous and not so famous, were Rosemary's friends and champions as she struggled to regain her balance after Stephen's death. Her salvation came, naturally enough, in the literary world. The early promise in her work for the *Herald Tribune* in Paris and the columns for American magazines in the 1920s had resurfaced as she collaborated with Stephen on a volume of verse for young people, *A Book of Americans*. Her poem in that book, "Nancy Hanks," drew the most critical and popular applause of all the poems. After 1943 she kept her vow to dedicate herself to perpetuate the memory of her husband and his work. John Farrar, still the "log-roller," recommended her for the board of the Book of the Month Club, and thereafter she became an important figure in literary circles in her own right. Until her death from cancer in 1962, she maintained the lovely house where she and Stephen had lived in Stonington, Connecticut.

Notes

1. INTRODUCTIONS

1. Stephen Vincent Benét (hereafter cited as SVB) to Laura Benét (hereafter cited as LB), Oct. 14, [1940].

2. *Time*, Nov. 4, 1940.

3. Leonard Bacon, *Semi-centennial* (New York: Harper, 1939), 163.

4. Frances Rose Benét (hereafter cited as FRB) to William Rose Benét (hereafter cited as WRB), Feb. 1907.

5. Charles A. Fenton, *Stephen Vincent Benét: The Life and Times of an American Man of Letters, 1898-1943* (New Haven, Conn.: Yale University Press, 1958), 109.

2. PARIS AND LOVE

1. Rosemary Carr Benét (hereafter cited as RCB) to Dr. Rachel Hickey Carr (hereafter cited as RHC), Dec. 13, 1919.

2. RCB to Family, June 11, 1920.

3. RCB to Family, Nov. 7, 1920.

4. Douglas Moore, talk on the Canadian Broadcast Channel (CBC), June 17, 1953. A transcript is in the Benét archives at the Beinecke Library.

5. Ibid.

6. RCB to Family, Dec. 28, 1920.

7. Walter de la Mare, *Collected Poems, 1901-1918* (New York: Henry Holt, 1920), 10.

8. RCB to RHC, Jan. 18, 1921.

9. SVB, *Selected Letters of Stephen Vincent Benét*, ed. Charles Fenton (New Haven, Conn.: Yale University Press, 1960), 54.

10. RCB to RHC, June 30, 1921.

3. AT HOME

1. Catharine Hopkins (hereafter cited as CH) to RCB, Sept. 1, [1921].

2. SVB to RCB, [Oct. 1921], in SVB, *Selected Letters,* 93–95.

3. WRB, *The Dust Which Is God* (New York: Dodd, Mead, 1941), 344.

4. *New York Times,* July 28, 1929.

5. Richard Myers (hereafter cited as REM) to SVB and RCB, Nov. 10, 1921.

6. RCB to Family, Nov. 28, 1921.

7. RCB to Family, Dec. 8, 1921.

4. MARRIAGE AND FAMILIES

1. REM to Dear Children, Jan. 12, 1922.

2. SVB to RCB, [June 1922].

3. Kathleen Norris, *Butterfly* (New York: A. L. Burt, 1923), 74–75.

4. REM to SVB, Sept. 14, 1921.

5. REM to SVB, July 27, 1922.

6. Scott Fitzgerald, *Letters of F. Scott Fitzgerald,* ed. Andrew Turnbull (New York: Charles Scribner's Sons, 1963), 172.

7. SVB, *James Shore's Daughter* (Garden City, N.Y.: Doubleday, Doran, 1935), 203.

8. REM to RCB, Nov. 27, 1922.

9. RCB to RHC, Dec. 19, 1922.

5. COMPLICATIONS

1. RCB to RHC, Jan. 21, 1923.

2. Col. James Walker Benét (hereafter cited as JWB) to SVB, Aug. 22, 1923.

3. RCB to CH, Jan. 22, [1923].

4. REM to SVB and RCB, Feb. 19, 1923.

5. Margaret Cox Benét to FRB, April 12, 1923.

6. REM to Stephen and Jane, June 27, 1923.

7. FRB to EW, March 4, 1923.

8. Moore, talk on the Canadian Broadcast Channel.

9. William Rose to FRB and LB, July 22, 1923.

10. RCB to RHC, July 26, 1923.

11. EW to RCB, Sept. 29, 1923.

12. Stanley Olson, *Elinor Wylie: A Life Apart* (New York: Dial, 1979), 225.

13. CH to REM, n.d.

14. Edmund Wilson, *The Twenties,* introduction by Leon Edel (New York: Farrar, Straus and Giroux, 1975), 78–79.

15. James Branch Cabell, *Some of Us: An Essay in Epitaphs* (New York: Robert M. McBride, 1930), 24.

16. JWB to SVB, Oct. 27, 1923.

17. Rosemary Benét Dawson to Stanley Olson, Feb. 12, 1975, Mugar Memorial Library, Boston University.

6 . BABY

1. RCB to Dick and Alice Lee, Feb. 29, [1924].

2. RCB to RHC, April 1, 1924.

3. SVB to Alice Lee and REM, [April 14, 1924].

4. RHC to RCB, Nov. 6. 1924.

5. RCB to Mother and Father, Nov. 6, 1924.

6. RCB to RHC, Nov. 1, 1924.

7. *Bookman,* June 1, 1927.

8. REM to SVB, Nov. 1, 1924.

7 . TRAGEDY

1. Elinor Wylie (hereafter cited as EW) to RCB, Jan. 27, 1925.

2. EW, *Selected Works of Elinor Wylie,* ed. Evelyn Helmick Hively (Kent, Ohio: Kent State University Press, 2005), 125.

3. RCB to RHC, March 31, 1925.

4. EW to Blanche Knopf, Sept. 12, [1925], Harry Ransom Humanities Research Center, University of Texas at Austin, in Olson, *Elinor Wylie,* 262.

5. WRB to FRB, Aug. 23, 1925.

6. FRB to LB, Sept. 16, 1925.

7. REM to SVB and RCB, Oct. 13, 1925.

8. REM to SVB, Jan. 13, 1926.

9. FRB to LB, Nov. 29, 1925.

10. F. Scott Fitzgerald, *A Life in Letters,* ed. Matthew Bruccoli (New York: Charles Scribner's Sons, 1994), 134.

11. FRB to WRB, Jan. 1, 1926.

8. PARIS ENCORE

1. CH to ALM, Aug. 24, [1923].
2. RCB to RHC and Thomas Carr, April 10, 1926.
3. RCB to RHC, April 20, 1926.
4. SVB to RCB, May 27, 1926.
5. EW to RCB, Aug. 8, 1926.

9. PRODUCTIVE DAYS

1. FRB to RCB, [March 1927].
2. FRB to LB, April 24, [1927].
3. JWB to SVB, June 15, [1927].
4. RCB to RHC, June 2, [1927].
5. RCB to RHC, May 22, 1927.
6. JWB to SVB, June 15, [1927].
7. JWB to SVB, June 15, [1927].
8. FRB to WRB, June 13, 1927.
9. FRB to SVB, June 3, 1927.
10. *Bookman,* June 1, 1927, 406.
11. *Saturday Review of Literature,* Nov. 1, 1941, 23.
12. RCB to RHC, Aug. 29, 1927.
13. RHC to RCB, Aug. 19, 1927.
14. RCB to RHC, Sept.16, 1927.
15. RCB to RHC, Aug. 23, 1927.
16. FRB to SVB, n.d.

10. PAIN AND GRIEF

1. SVB, *James Shore's Daughter,* 203.
2. SVB to John Farrar, May 6, 1928.
3. SVB to John Farrar, June [17], 1928.
4. RHC to RCB, June 1, 1928.
5. SVB to John Farrar, July 14, 1928.
6. RCB to RHC, Aug. 2, 1928.
7. WRB, *The Dust Which Is God,* 360.
8. RCB to RHC, Dec. 2, [1928].

9. RCB to WRB, Dec. 18, 1928.

10. Jean Gould, *The Poet and Her Book: A Biography of Edna St. Vincent Millay* (New York: Dodd, Mead, 1969), 193.

11. Douglas Moore to SVB & RCB, Dec. 18, [1928].

12. FRB to RHC, Jan. 11, [1929]. Letter is dated 1928.

13. RHC to FRB, Jan. 17, 1929.

11. FROM PARIS TO NEW YORK

1. RCB to RHC, March 8, 1931.

2. Caroline Lovett to Mrs. Howard Meriwether Lovett, July 19, 1929.

3. FRB to SVB, July 18, 1929.

4. RHC to RCB, March 10, [1929].

5. RCB to REM, Jan. 1, 1930.

12. END OF A DECADE

1. RCB to REM, Jan. 16, 1930.

2. RHC to RCB, Nov. 16, 1929.

3. RHC to RCB, March 16, 1930.

13. GOOD-BYES

1. Rosemary's entry at the end of Stephen's diary has been transcribed and is found in the Rosemary Benét collection in the Yale Collection of American Literature in the Beinecke Rare Book and Manuscript Library.

2. Virgilia Paulding to Josephine Gregory, Aug. 1952, private papers of Thomas Carr Benét.

3. Rachel Benét Lewis, "I Only Drank When I Needed It," *McCall's*, Aug. 1977, 112, 121, 188.

Excerpts from Writing by Rosemary Carr Benét
1926 to 1931

Immediately after her year at the École Normale Supérieure de Sèvres, Rosemary began to work as a journalist, first at a magazine for Americans, called *Welcome*, then more seriously at the Cross-Atlantic Newspaper Service. Within months, she was offered a position with the European edition of the *Chicago Tribune*, where her talent impressed the director, and her by-line appeared regularly. But she left France in 1922 to return to the United States with Stephen, whose work was beginning to attract attention.

The years between residencies in Paris brought marriage, responsibilities, and loss of the time and spirit needed to create. Only to her close friend, Catharine Hopkins, could she confide her disappointment and resentment at having to sacrifice her own opportunity for writing in order to meet the demands of others. Later, when she returned to live permanently in New York after 1929, she produced some of the work that demonstrated her abilities, as she collaborated with Stephen on *A Book of Americans, Captain Kidd,* and *Johnny Appleseed,* where she was listed as the first author. She translated Colette's *The Gentle Libertine* in 1931 and *A Lesson in Love* in 1932 for Farrar and Rinehart, and Maurois' *Fatapoufs and Thinifers* in 1940 for Henry Holt.

But her opportunities and enthusiasm for writing had returned previously when the Benéts returned to France in 1926. The best of American magazines, among them, *Harper's Bazaar, Vogue,* and the *New Yorker,* published her poetry and her comments on French fashion and manners. In the fall of 1927, the ever-helpful Richard Myers used his influence to find her a position as the Paris correspondent for *Town and Country,* a glossy, sophisticated New York periodical. Twice each month Rosemary wrote a full page of "Our Paris Letter," with each page graced by a photograph of

Parisian couture or society members. Her connection with those prominent Americans in Paris, Stephen's Uncle Laurence and Aunt Margaret, undoubtedly gave her access to information and gossip that helped make the columns interesting. But her own clever, ironic view of the Parisian scene made them lively and funny.

Her views were personal and her tone was familiar, but the subjects were those dear to French hearts and fascinating to the American readers of glossy magazines—fashion, culture, the comings and goings of the upper crust. The excerpts reprinted here, about one-third of each month's column, have been chosen because they reveal something of the history and the people of the time, capture the spirit of the city, or illuminate the lives of the Benéts and their friends.

There are inconsistencies in grammar and spelling that appear just as they were printed, and French words are italicized only sometimes. The copy, then, is as Rosemary wrote it or as her editors chose to publish it.

"Our Paris Letter,"
Town and Country, *November 1927 to June 1929*

November 1, 1927
There used to be seasons, just as there once were gourmets and devoted personal body servants, but they are no more. They have vanished like the great auk and the famous *neiges d'antan*. There was a London season and Paris season and a season for each of the resorts—a schedule as inflexible as a timetable. People stayed in place like the pieces in a chess game until it was time for the next move. Now they go flying off, according to the whim of the moment, or the weather. Life is no longer regulated by the calendar—a change to be wept at or praised, according to one's age and degree of conservatism.

Traditionally in the middle of summer, Paris should have been shuttered and swept bare. Everyone should have left it but tourists who regard the Tomb of Napoleon in all weathers and shopkeepers who pursue their trades in all seasons (except when they too put up the blinds and hop off to their natal farms). On the contrary, it was full of people who had run up from Deauville or were mid-way between Le Touquet and the Lido, or had simply found it cold and rainy in the country. They stayed a week or a month, went to the theater and the opening of their favorite dressmaker, and were caught unblushing and unashamed in the Ritz in mid-August.

Now in the late fall, when according to an even sterner tradition, everyone should be reinstated in Paris with his freshly dusted lares and penates about him, there are many laggards. The old houses have been opened and aired, the shutters swung back and the slip covers removed from the chairs in the salons. But the roads are still full of people skipping back and forth for a last country fling while the weather is fine.

The weather has come back as a topic conversationally—a melancholy one. People speculate gloomily as to whether the Seine will flood. It has been amply proved that the world cannot be deluged by forty days and forty nights of rain since it has survived several months of it here. Looking back over the summer with a pessimistic autumnal eye, one decides the rain *did* spoil all the resorts in spite of reports to the contrary. Only the Lido and Riviera escaped. The one consolation in a sea of rain is that the wine crop prospered and is reported excellent, "equal or better than in 1926, with a probable total of fifty million hectoliters."

But to get back to Paris. An innovation in art exhibits was the "salon de l'escalier," held on a stairway in Theatre des Champs-Elysees in the Avenue Montaigne. It wound up one hundred steps and over ten landings and may presage a combination of art with exercise. Certainly many ladies who have not for years climbed one hundred stairs or seen the second balcony of a theater will do so in the interest of art. Think of the possibilities of the development of this aesthetic-athletic wedding! The expositions in the Grand Palais could be a kind of field day with races and hurdles to relieve the monotony of several miles of pictures. However, the salon de l'escalier was more noteworthy because of the way it was hung than for what was hung therein. The exhibition was modern and mediocre and showed several of the more untidy realists. Only the sculptures of Roy Sheldon, a young American, were excellent. He exhibited some twenty pieces and four were wisely placed near the entrance to tempt people to the less interesting works of art above, and the fatigue of the stairs. His sculptured animals are delightful, done in various adapted mediums; the medium chosen, I suppose, to suit each animal nature. Thus the penguin appears appropriately in Norwegian granite, a kangaroo, giraffe and crane in bronze, an elephant in Belgian granite, a monkey in ebony and a duck in lacquered wood. To show how really modern the exhibit was, the names of the exhibitors in the catalogue were all spelled with small letters, frans masereel, dora bianka, l.r. antral. george grosz, etc. I can never see why this is supposed to give a cachet of modernity.

Paul Poiret plans a fall trip to America and by this time should be in New York. I wonder how far his gospel of individuality in dress will prove convincing. More than any other couturier he dislikes uniformity and conventionality and the usual. Not for him is our repetition of one popular model in black or beige on old and young and fat and thin, That may make for fewer badly dressed people, but not enough perfectly dressed ones for his taste. Each woman, he thinks, should dress distinctively, with personality, in an interesting way. And if possible not like anyone else. He is at present predicting trousers as a feminine style development, which evokes groans from most of his followers. Why should women wear anything so ugly as trousers? His answer is that they are comfortable and may be beautiful. In his fall collection he shows several variations—mostly with evening dresses. They range from soft bloomery ones, hardly visible under wide skirts, to a taffeta skirt that buttons with tabs about the ankles. I should scoff at this revolutionary idea except that I remember that years ago he predicted short hair as the coming fashion. In a day with pompadours and ringlets and hair that was measured by quantity not quality, that seemed absurd. But where are the Sutherland sisters and the hair that reached to the knees now? So perhaps he is equally prophetic with trousers.

Two of the most interesting models in his collections have historical connections. A beautiful evening wrap is *Charles VII* and is on supple scarlet velvet with flowing sleeves and gathered fullness. *Vermeer* is a picturesque evening dress of black velvet with wide chiffon sleeves and a white satin underskirt, a costume worthy of an early Flemish painter. They both show the new interest in velvet and continued popularity of the picturesque mode, particularly for evening.

At Poiret's too—this time in the decorating part downstairs—I saw a very modern straw screen. The panels are made of brightly colored wide shiny straw in a brilliant flower design. It is like the modern straw-paneled suite he designed for the *Ile-de-France.*

November 15, 1927
As soon as the gardens begin to bloom with dahlias and purple asters a crop of exhibitions springs up. They are as certain a fall harvest as the silvery Peter's Pence that grows every autumn in florists' windows, and this year they are unusually numerous. At the present moment we are ridden by them. The Motor Show at the Grand Palais and the international photograph exhibit in the Rue de Clichy are perhaps the most important. But there is also a Food and Wine Exhibition at Magic City that is reported a paradise for gourmets; a leather exhibition near the Porte de Versailles and an exhibition of chrysanthemums in Cours la Reine. An exhibit of the "Arts of Hairdressing and Perfumery" is announced for the end of this month in Palm House of the Jardin d'Acclimatation, probably to the intense surprise of the surrounding elephants and bears and camels. The nearby foxes I hope will be sprayed with Coty, for they are the most malodorous animals in Paris. An exhibition of mushrooms has been gaily going on in the Musee d'Hygiene in the Boulevard Sebastopol. Dozens of mushrooms are classed as *non comestible, très bon comestible, indigeste, mortelle* and *pathogène.* People hasten up to match the suspicious ones they have found in country woods.

It is in the wide open spaces between seasons that the mode calmly appears. In August and February it is created. Exhausted designers work at top speed, wishing they had six hands and four feet. Mannequins are harried. Buyers are hag-ridden that a rival may become clairvoyant before them. Everything is hectic and uncertain. Now, two months later, the clients have done their share of deciding. The result of all this work and fret is seen, worn at the races at Longchamp, or at tea or out dining in Paris. One sees not a prophecy of what is to be worn, but what is actually being worn. They do not always agree.

Black is smart. Velvet is the favorite material, particularly for afternoon and evening wear. If colors are worn in street clothes they are apt to be one of the brown tones, shading out through the lighter putty and beige. A soft green is also sometimes seen. But black is the favorite. Black, blacker. At the Prix de l'Arc de Triomphe the perfect weather brought out an even larger crowd than for the Grand Prix. The entire scene could have been done by an etcher with little loss of color. It was strikingly black and white, black velvet coats, black satin ensembles, wide collars of black and white fox.

Yet all this black in no way suggests mourning. The materials are never dull or thick. Velvet and satin give a shiny surface; the blackness is lightened by a flower or a crystal necklace. The line of the gown is gayer and more subtle than even the most casual mourning.

Paris, with its interest in detail, loves accessories, and particularly this season since they are used to lighten the scheme of blackness. Chanel sponsors the new mode for crystal jewels—long strings of flat stones set in silvery metal. Sometimes they are brilliants (or diamonds, if you insist), but usually crystals in colors shading through rose, lavender and blue. They are more becoming than the short, stocky pearl necklaces once in vogue. They possess the added charm of color and the fact that they escape the ignominy of imitation, being frankly what they seem, semi-precious stones. Patou sponsors large flat jewels, often topazes or amethysts, holding a drapery at the side of a gown. Lanvin approves wide black velvet dog collars for evening. Jewelers have adapted these ideas variously. The side interests of the mode grow broader each day. Soon couturiers will be designing motors to match their gowns.

Another popular accessory is the felt bag made to match the small felt hats that are so much worn. It is strange no one thought of this before, since felt is an excellent bag material, and the idea of gloves, stockings, bag and hat being in harmony has become a convention.

A new house worth watching, or rather an old house with a new name is Brialix. They were once Madeleine and Madeleine, later Anna, and finally, Brialix. They still inhabit the spacious salons of Madeleine and Madeleine in the Champs Elysées. They emphasize a new color—pink and its variants, sometimes rose, sometimes salmon, sometimes a pale flesh tint; very often combined with black. Their afternoon dresses have narrow bands, finely made, almost exclusively for trimming.

December 1, 1927
King Faud of Egypt is our latest royal visitor. He has been much entertained, officially and informally. Many of the American colony saw him at a large dinner and reception at the Union Interalliée. He is French in sympathy. His Queen Mazli is the great-granddaughter of a French officer, Captain Sèves, who was one of the organizers of the Egyptian army. His daughter is the wife of the Egyptian minister in Paris, Fakhry Pacha. The bright green flag with the crescent moon is rampant and gentlemen in fezzes (what is the plural?) are stared at solemnly.

That reminds me that a few weeks ago, when the Japanese prince was in Paris dedicating a student hostel, I saw a most amusing incident. An unfortunate little Chinese couple decided to walk along the Rue de Rivoli, aimlessly looking in windows near the Maurice, famous for housing royalty. The rumor sprang up that here was the Japanese prince and princess. Immediately a good-natured crowd collected, shoving and pointing and staring, content to be rubbing elbows in the common pursuit of a celebrity. The bewildered Orientals, who were no more Japanese royalty than the crowd watching them, hastily summoned a taxi and fled. Paris loves to stalk celebrities and now the streets are full of them.

Worth made the gowns for the wedding of Anne of France, daughter of the pretender, the Duc de Guise, and the Duc des Pouilles. The lovely Anne, who is really regal as are few princesses, wore a beautifully simple gown and magnificent lace veil, so long that it was carried by six pages. She gave all the little girls who worked on her trousseau a small silver box with an inscription. Her vendeuse was invited to the nuptials in Naples. All in the best royal tradition. It is said also that by order of the court it was decreed that only the bride should wear white; all the other ladies present, including the bridesmaids, wore colored gowns. This is a new monopoly.

M. Mussolini came to the civil ceremony as notary for the crown. The witnesses were the King of Spain and the heir apparent of Italy for the bride, and the King of Italy and the Duc de Genes for the groom.

The Maharajah of Kapurthala, who is such a statuesque figure at the races and at Ciro's, has left Paris for India to celebrate the fiftieth—he succeeded at the age of five—anniversary of his reign. Before leaving he gave fifty thousand francs to the poor of Paris.

That reminds me of the lady at the races who, on having The Aga Khan pointed out asked if he was related to Otto Kahn. But enough of kings and queens. They are less interesting than jacks and knaves.

Now is the moment for furs, not because of the weather, which has been temperate, but because of vanity, which is intemperate. The two smartest furs for coats are undoubtedly summer ermine and breitschwantz, with shaved lamb and caracul one lap behind. Summer ermine keeps its popularity because of its softness; it can be draped like a material and is endless in its adaptations. I saw a beautiful coat of this fur at Longchamps, with a becoming sloping shoulder line, loose puff sleeves drawn into tighter cuffs, and a scarf knotted under the chin like a muffler. Such drapable quality is remarkable in fur. Breitschwantz is often stunningly combined with silver fox. Another coat I saw worn at Longchamps and later identified as coming from Lanvin was of gray shaved lamb bordered with a narrow band of black in the same fur down the front, around the high military collar and on the cuff.

Worth, in his mid-season collection, had some timely fur ideas. He is using small fur scarves on his coats that are almost like mufflers. There is an opening slit on one side of the collar and the other end of the fur scarf loops through tightly and is thrown over the shoulder. This is both smart and warm. Evidently a soft fur is used—summer ermine, honey-colored moleskin or ermines's poor relation, rabbit. He also trimmed a seal coat effectively with a rolling collar and round ball-cuffs of nutria. For evening he has a beautiful wrap of white ermine, the narrow skins cleverly sewed to make a curved shoulder line in back. It would not be possible to mention this collection without noting his emphasis on a new color for street and sports things, a soft gray-green, the color of the sea.

January 1, 1928

About the time the Christmas tree is shedding its needles untidily and the holiday greeting cards lie in a dusty, neglected mound, people begin to migrate. They look at railroad timetables. They wonder if it really is warm somewhere else. Here in Paris there are fewer cards but even more departures. One's banker and bondsalesman and laundryman do not send "wishes for your patronage in the new year as in the old." Instead, the domestic staffs line up for their yearly étrennes. The mailman knocks at the door with a hopeful gleam in his eye, waiting for his contribution. Not only the mailman. Packages, telegrams, registered letters, all assume human forms in search of New Year's presents. Étrennes bestowed, people are off to St. Moritz for winter sports. Or to the Midi. Mimosa comes into the flower markets. Now mimosa is an ugly plant, loved only by French people from the south. It is ungraceful with its stiff yellow balls. It has a dusty smell and makes one sneeze. But it possesses great powers of suggestion. It suddenly brings to mind the Riviera and the fields around Cannes and Grasse. I am sure it is responsible for more of the traffic southward than travel pamphlets.

Last week I helped outfit some people who were leaving for central Africa in search of neighboring lions and gorillas. They spent hectic days rushing about looking for water filters and little pocket mirrors to give natives who will come miles in search of a looking glass, and other essentials to life in the desert. Their guide, a seasoned African explorer wept over the difficulty of assembling equipment in Paris. In London or Brussels outfitting an expedition to the Congo is an everyday matter. There is no surprise about it. You get a complete kit from strange big-game bullets to toys to charm chieftains. If your winter migration is any place *but* Africa, however, Paris is ready for you. The couturiers have been concentrating on sports clothes and will outfit you for resorts, hot or cold, as you choose, skiing or surf-bathing.

Jane Regny's specialty is sports clothes. The reason this house has made such a success with its sport things is that they are simple in line, attractive and practical. Perhaps I should put practical first. But I do not use the word in its dreary tweedy sense. When there are capes, they are there for warmth. They may also add smartness of line, but that is incidental. The skiing things are sturdy and warm. The golf and tennis dresses easy to move in. Elemental, perhaps, but too often forgotten.

Madeleine Vionnet is an artist at whatever she turns her hand to—evening gowns, fur coats, street clothes. I was not surprised to find that her distinguished collection includes some excellent sports things. They are marked by her usual elegant simplicity. They are oftenest a coat and dress ensemble—a tweed coat for traveling, fairly long and flaring at the hem, trimmed with beaver or broadtail or some other drapable fur. The dress is in crepe de chine, frequently in a warm bois de rose shade. Her classic lines are accentuated by faggoting, hemstitching, or tucking. Often the fine handwork makes a sun-ray design in the front of the dress. The crepe de chine dresses are her masterpieces, simple elegant in line, yet most intricately made. She has a practical ensemble for skiing. And fur coats that make one almost decide to go to a more rigorous climate than Palm Beach, after all.

January 15, 1928

The first of the literary prizes have fluttered down on the elect like manna from heaven, modern manna in form of certified checks. As a result of this literary Tap Day, M. Maurice Bedel has won the Prix Goncourt for his book "Jerome, 60° de Latitude Nord." The Prix Femina goes to Mademoiselle Marie Le France for "Grand Louis l'Innocent." The former work describes Norway and will therefore be unpleasing to Norwegians. Mademoiselle Le Franc's work is more safely though gloomily set in Brittany. The author, who is in Canada, when informed of her luck cabled back laconically the one word "Chic." The Prix Goncourt has a limiting clause, by the way. It is for the conventional "best book"—but the best book in the tradition of the Goncourts; that is to say, a work of uncompromising realism. Sometimes it comes to unknown authors, making them famous overnight. Its most illustrious past protégés are Farrière and Proust. A check, a bright colored paper around the novel, large sales, fame. Among the candidates this year was Julian Green for his book "Adrienne Mesurat." Mr. Green is a young American who has lived most of his life in Paris and who writes in French.

A most amusing play, "Vient de Paraitre," which has just come on, exploits book prizes. It is by Edmond Bourdet, author of the sensational "La Prisonnière," produced last year in New York. The hero, a completely unknown author, wins the Prix Zola and with fame acquires literary and domestic inhibitions. According to M. Lucien Descaves, a member of the Goncourt committee, the play is founded on reality. One year the prize went to a novelist from Niort, who had previously sold exactly three copies of his work. Another year, it went to someone whose address was so completely unknown that only by the aid of frantic searching in the telephone book was he informed of his good fortune. The Bourdet play gives away many secrets of the literary trade, including the tricks of profiteering publishers.

André Maurois, back on the *Ile de France* from a tour of America, spoke enthusiastically of his trip. He has been widely interviewed and, like Lindbergh, has managed at all times to say pleasant, intelligent and honest things without appearing to be consciously diplomatic. Discriminating praise, not platitudes, came even when he was interviewed at midnight before leaving the boat. He liked America and is going back next year to lecture at Princeton, which is good news.

One of the few American guests who attended the ball given by the Duchesse de Gramont at the Château de Vallière gave me an interesting account of it. The château dates from François I and has richly carved oak boiseries and yellow damask walls and superb crystal chandeliers. Against this ancient background were the most modern of costumes—no brocaded dresses, no tiaras. All the dresses were simple in line, many silver and white, a few lace ones such as Chanel makes, with one end forming a scarf, many of softly draped velvet, chiffon or satin entirely untrimmed, short and smart. A "défilé Venitien" was the divertissement of the evening. Twenty or more guests took part in a carefully planned tableau. This was pleasantly but mildly received. An impromptu modern dance by two debutantes to jazz improvised by some of the guests hastily blacked up, was the real hit of the evening. The ancestral portraits watched while Mademoiselle Faucigny Lucinge and Mademoiselle Thion de La Chaume did the Charleston. The latter, by the way, is an excellent golfer as well as a dancer—the Women's Champion of France.

Twice a year at the tag end of the season, the big dressmaking houses have sales. They clear out their cupboards and have a grand "clarin' up." Dresses are sold for a sixth to a tenth of their regular price—furs, bits of material—everything is thrown in. The aristocratic strongholds suddenly become soviet states for one day. For the couturiers are the remnant of old aristocratic tradition. It is a couturier, for instance, who keeps the late Czarina's private dressing-room just as she left it, untouched, unused. Where else, in trade or out, do you find such sentiment? And many a lady who would risk going to a tea with rain spotted stocking or a chance rip in her glove, thinks timidly of the keen eye of her vendeuse. But on one day all is changed. The splendid lynx-eyed door attendants look the other way in melancholy, while streams of bargain hunters rush feverishly by. It is a most amusing scene. Ladies seize hold of the same dress and pull. The strongest wins, if the dress does not crack first. Most of the houses remove their labels from the gowns before the holocaust, thus washing their hands of the whole affair. The haughtier houses will not even allow their dressing rooms to be polluted by the rabble—so the dresses are held up appraisingly in full view of the surrounding amateurs of bargains. Some of the regular clientele come back, to buy the one dress their conscience would not let them have. Many smart French women with mannequin figures manage by these sales to dress themselves with pre-war elegance in spite of post-war incomes. Some are just inveterate bargain hunters.

February 1, 1928

The hats that bloom in the spring, tra-la, unlike Messrs. Gilbert and Sullivan's flowers, have a great deal to do with the face. It is a little early yet to speculate about them. Rather like pulling a flower up by its roots and saying determinedly, "This will be a pansy." However, once it is definitely a pansy, or an onion, it is no fun to speculate. So let us, aided by the modistes, hazard a few prophecies.

The simple felt hat, which has had more than the traditional two terms as a successful candidate, is due to be replaced by something more elaborate. Do not wince at the word elaborate. It means scant and discreet trimming and a greater variety of material—that's all. Head sizes are still small. Trimming is simple. But modistes must have a change some time. There is no scope to a felt cloche with a ribbon band once it has been done in a variety of colors—and they have been making them for years. Variety is a spice which hatmakers pray for. But probably (I add skeptically), prophecy or not, we will all be ordering simple felt hats all over again.

Suzanne Talbot is doing interesting things with veils—short voilettes that come just to the end of the nose. Those nose veils are much seen in plain tulle or large-meshed veiling ending in a border of fine black dots. They are becomingly mysterious and lack the stuffy disadvantages of the old-fashioned all-over kind. They may presage a return, however, to the longer trailing ones. Talbot also suggests rose and black as a happy hat combination; and, to prove it, showed me a close-fitting straw called Thaïs. The rose color was inset on the sides; the top and close-fitting back were of black. This was also developed in the same color and material, but with the addition of a small brim. Spring and sunshine bring back brims as inevitably as crocuses.

The Riviera is pleasantly warm and crowded according to latest reports. One has to book weeks in advance on the famous Blue Train. During our late cold spell, when snow fell in the Midi for the first time in years, the excellent press agent, who had been up to that moment expatiating on the joys of the sunlight, rose to the occasion, speaking of the "curious and beautiful effect formed by the snow on the palms, an unusual treat for the visitors." The celebrities are as varied as possible. There are many tennis stars down for the tournaments. . . . Near St. Jean Cap Ferrat, the so-called "new Riviera," there is a literary colony. Somerset Maugham, Gilbert Frankau, Captain and Mrs. H. M. Harwood, the latter better known as Miss Tennyson Jess, Paul Geraldy and Victor Margueritte are all neighbors.

The port at Monaco is full of yachts. There are many American and British ones. Among the American contingent are Mr. A. K. Macomber's *Crusader,* Mrs. Alexander S. Cochran's three-masted schooner, *Vira* (a new vessel), Mr. Franklin Singer's *Xarifa,* and the Countess Zbrowska's boat, *Gray Mist.* Already there is much talk of the yacht races from New York to San Sebastian next July for the cups offered by the Spanish King and Queen. Many of the yachts now anchored near Monte Carlo will be going back for that.

February 15, 1928
People who haven't been in Paris for a few months will find several changes. I never can decide whether it changes more or less than any other city. There are never miles of torn-up disemboweled streets. Coming back after an absence, it is comfortingly the same. Yet each change rouses such a storm of comment here, such eager discussion—so jealously is the city's appearance guarded by its inhabitants—that the alteration becomes magnified. Let us hope *plus ça change, plus c'est la même chose.*

For instance, a new bridge is nearly done, the Pont de la Tournelle, running from the Ile Saint Louis to the left bank of the Seine. A question rose about the location of a statue on the bridge. Newspapers, which have columns devoted to the care and restoration of the city's glories have argued about it. Should the statue of Sainte Geneviève look west towards Notre Dame, or should she face the Pont de Sully to the east? Should there be two statues for symmetry? How about the vista? Every variant of pedestal and location has been suggested. The last verdict I have heard is that Landowski, the sculptor thinks the saint should look towards Notre Dame. And as a block of granite is to be put up and he is to carve the statue there himself, he seems to have the final word to say about it.

The Hotel de Massa, a landmark at the Champs Elysées and the Rue de la Poetie has been carried stone by stone to the Observatory gardens where it will be rebuilt to house a literary society. It is not only Americans who move houses. It vanished a cartload at a time, each stone carefully numbered. It is too bad to have it go for it was almost the last stronghold against the march of business up the avenue. Most of the other old houses have capitulated for one story at least to motor cars or perfumes or other lures of modern business. The Hotel de Massa was not, comparatively so very old; it was built about 1785. Napoleon was received there in 1804 by Count Marescalchi. There was a pleasant suggestion of Restoration balls about its long windows and formal garden, which will missed.

Another change which will come more gradually but will be far reaching, is that no more chestnut trees will be planted in Paris. The chestnut is a delicate tree, unfitted for the strain of a modern Paris existence. It is like a mid-Victorian heroine, beautiful but not hardy enough for modern life. Dust and tar and gasoline fumes blight it as they do all velvety-leaved trees. As soon as one dies it is to be replaced by a more stalwart tree, plane or linden. Fortunately it will be a long time before the chestnut will vanish, for this tree with its cone-shaped blossoms like Christmas tree candles and its arching branches, is typical of Paris. Even to the variety called the "vingt mars" because it is supposed to bloom then, though it rarely blooms until the middle of April.

Antiquing is as much of an all-year-round sport as ever. Antique bargains are as rare as finding pearls in oyster, or diamond bracelets in taxis. Still, people do find both. This hope always adds zest to my eating of oysters or taking taxis, otherwise, I find, rather dull occupations. I hear that old French rustic furniture and early Empire, which was once an âge ingrat and could be picked up for little, is becoming popular and hence expensive. It is in demand partly because it mixes better with early American than the more ornate formal periods.

Lustres one sees everywhere. Crystal candlesticks adorn antique shop and electrical shop alike and almost every blind that is not drawn at six shows a crystal chandelier shining and gleaming. A few years ago the rosettes, prisms, and pear-shaped drops of lustres were considered worthless and taken apart and given to children in the nursery to hang. Now the broken fragments so desecrated are picked up and carefully mended to be proudly reinstated in the salon.

There are several stock stories one runs across antiquing. People who bought a desk and found valuable papers or coins in a secret drawer. An amber necklace bought for little in Marseilles is found to contain initials showing it had been given by Napoleon to Josephine. There are variants of these two. The realities are quite as astonishing. I know someone who picked up in Spain for a few coins a volume mixed in with a heap of old English books. It was a book with an inscription that Keats had given to his sister. Not long ago an American found the original manuscript of Oscar Wilde's Salomé in a Montmartre bookshop. And one rainy day this year—the rainy day all amateurs of antiques pray for—an authentic Louis XIV bed was bought at auction at the Hotel Drouot for six francs, plus eighty-five centimes tax. It had been a long day of miscellaneous sales. The dealers were preoccupied. The bed was started at five francs—six was bid and got it. I need not add that this does not happen often. Another day from the collection of old books by M. Gabriel Hanotaux, the Academician, an ivory-bound book, ornamented with fleur de lys believed to have been a present from Gabrielle d'Estrées to Henri IV, went for a modest sum. Keen bidding was roused over a small volume containing Corneille's Andromede, bearing the names of the cast in the handwriting of Molière. It went to a private collector, though one of the big libraries tried to secure it for the nation.

March 1, 1928

The opening of a big dressmaking house is increasingly like the first night of a play. More and more of the collections are first shown at night. People come in evening dress (last season's, inevitably). There are words and music—elaborately printed programs and an orchestra moaning softly while the mannequins pass. Fashion critics, like dramatic critics, come with weary, jaded, all-seeing eyes. Celebrities are pointed out in a whisper. The notables are more apt to be the head of a famous silk or woolen industry than the latest author of a best seller, or an actress dressed by the house, and an ambassador. Still they are just as well-known in this field. There is the same nervousness that pervades the first night of a play, the prick of excitement that shakes the all-star cast and the usher alike, and the head vendeuse and the smallest trottin. Will it go over well? At the end there is the same instant response from the audience if the collection is a success—the real applause that cannot be simulated by any claque. And where is the head of house during this elaborate gala? Like the playwright, he is skulking or exultant depending on temperament. I know one playwright who seldom goes to a first night, or if he does, hides in the top gallery.

Others wait alert and bold, murmuring metaphors, hopeful that they may be called for a curtain speech. So the designer may emerge expansive and smiling, or pale and distraught. But neither the excellence of the play nor the collection have anything to do with that.

The season is still young. Many of the big houses are yet to have their openings, which run late this year. Their discoveries are unseen and un-sung. From those who have already shown the collections the following new ideas are gleaned: The waist line is slightly higher, more nearly the normal line. The designers are clever about this change. The tendency is inevitably toward the higher line, but the move must not be made abrupt-ly. There can be no suggestion of tightness. At the word stays, the modern woman would rebel. But the new line, if it is also comfortable and grace-ful, interests her. One designer prophesies we will soon be back at the 1860 line, but that is too reactionary.

Skirts are a little longer. Skirt hems are still gracefully irregular and tend to be longer in back than in front for evening. Colors vary with the designer. Jane Regny is using bright ones, for instance, and Lucien Lelong pastel shades, and a silver gray. The silhouette is primarily youthful.

Jane Regny's newest idea is the horoscope dress. At her opening she gave out a charmingly bound book containing an essay that she had writ-ten on the zodiac. A group of her dresses carry on this idea and are named for planets and the signs of the zodiac. They are colorful and noteworthy as an original conception. *Le Soleil,* for instance, is a two-piece white crêpe de chine dress with a golden disc at the shoulder and golden embroidered sun-rays running slantwise across the front. With these dresses are worn flat metal belts of gold or silver oval discs, which have the signs of the zodiac upon them. The collection in general is marked by vivid color and daring color combinations. Out of nearly two hundred models, I saw only one black dress and coat. A periwinkle blue and bright absinthe green are her favorite shades. Small patterned prints are popular. For evening she combines scarlets and wine reds and rose mauves admirably. The two-piece dress for evening continues to be stressed here.

This house is justly famous for its modern belts and buckles. Besides the new zodiac belt, there is an effective one made of flat gold coins, another of large gold nail heads, and a delightful crystal one for evening worn on a chiffon dress. The crystal links tinkled as the wearer moved—a charmingly cool sound for summer. The sweaters, another specialty, are, as usual, effective. They range from a very modern futuristic one called *Caligari*, to one with a large conventional fleur de lys pattern, appropriately named *Heraldique*.

March 15, 1928

It is increasingly difficult to write about fashion changes. There are fewer abrupt modifications, in the first place. The variations are slighter, more subtle and often have to do with nuances of line rather than radical differences in cut or material. It must have been easy enough to say "bustles have gone out and puffed sleeves have come in," or "hoop skirts are wider and it takes twelve yards of taffeta to make a dress."

Last season, someone said that women wore only sport clothes and evening gowns. The most important change of the new season is that this is no longer true. There is a definite afternoon mode. Sports clothes appear disguised in more elaborate materials, of course, but there is also a distinct feeling for a more formal gown.

Fulness is important in the new silhouette, particularly at the hemline. Sometimes this comes in circular flounces set in half-way down the skirt—a shortened version of the slim ruffled gowns once worn by Spanish dancers. The girdle remains slender. For evening, the uneven hemline is accentuated. Fulness becomes more pronounced in back, resulting in a suggestion of a modified bustle. Ruffles, frills, and fine pleats cannot be too much stressed. They are used endlessly to achieve modifications of the new line—diagonal, vertical, horizontal, semi-circular variants. Geometry is the newest study of the fashion experts. Circular hem flounces, frill, pleats, even ruffles have come in—yet simplicity of line remains. That is the keynote of the new mode.

The backs of gowns are apt to be more elaborate in details than fronts. All the floating shoulder ties and wing draperies and skirt flounces have a way of emphasizing themselves backwards.

As for materials—taffeta is increasingly important. Dark blue and black taffeta makes afternoon dresses, often with fine white ruffled collars and cuffs, the new feminine note. Worth, Patou, Premet and Lenief have good examples of this. A combination of two materials in the same design is new. Thus taffeta and chiffon, printed in an identical flower pattern, combine to make an evening dress. Among the favorite prints are the geometric and diagonal patterns (geometry again), and a large leaf design, all done in the original drawing by a fine penstroke which shows clearly on the crêpe de chine or chiffon. These are called pen line prints and are charming. As for wraps, the cape is omnipresent.

Paul Poiret can always be counted on for surprises. Whether one approves of his sartorial bombs or not, one must admit that he is an innovator. This time his hobby is the trouser skirt. Almost half the models in his collection have trousers—not only the discreet divided skirt hidden by a panel, suitable for sports, but uncompromising, flagrant trousers. They are apt to be soft draped ones for evening in chiffon or gold lace, but they also occur in tweed plus fours for daytime. Skirts (the conventional skirt!) when they appear in the collection, are long, full and graceful. The Oriental note—inherited supposedly by M. Poiret from a previous incarnation—influences color and embroidery. Many of the dresses have Arabian Nights names, Khedive, Pasha and the like. With each evening dress, he has designed a headdress, often a wreath of tulle or a bandeau of brilliants. In two evening dresses he goes unexpectedly back to the Directoire line. A long-skirted, tight, black picture dress called "Hommage à Rousseau," has a high waistline like the gowns worn by the Empress Josephine. This is shown effectively by a tall American mannequin and is a great contrast to her first appearance, when she wore a short coat, white shirtwaist, dark blue trousers-skirt and a monocle. Much lacquer red on dark blue is used by street wear. A hat made of isinglass is one of the curiosities of the collection. An amazing wedding dress called *marriage riche* has gold harem trousers and bodice and short tulle veil hung from the sleeves. The corresponding groom would masquerade as a sultan, I suppose.

Jenny's coats and street dresses I like best of the collection. The coats are simple, heavy tweeds with a youthfully flaring back. Her dresses, usually navy blue or black, have distinction. Box pleats, the bolero back, the Eton jacket, all appear. Jenny always manages to have a way with sleeves, making them interesting and various. One of her new ideas is a stiffly starched inner collar and cuff, ministerial in its severity, slipped beneath a dark one. Three half-inch-wide rolls of cloth, looped tightly about the neck, make her favorite collar. She is still using yellow effectively. There are fewer fringes than last season and less gold embroidery, though gold coins appear as the collar of a coat. This house likes short skirts. One small mannequin wore them just to her knee. For her evening gowns—all that is not gold at least glitters, and sometimes they are both glittering and golden.

May 15, 1928

The café tables are out on the sidewalks again. The chestnut trees, what are left of them, are in bloom. There are new orange awnings on apartment buildings. The uniformed English schoolboys, over in flocks like spring birds, have gone home, two by two, after moving in serious lines on the principal improving sights listed by Baedeker. The Parisians who went to Deauville for Easter are back. Election posters shout from every street corner. There is no more amusing or exciting reading than these texts, delightfully personal and acrid. Down with party A says one; it is leading us to perdition and anarchy. Party A calmly pastes its poster over the corner of this one, bitterly triumphant. Candidates, after the manner of candidates, are making sweet speeches. The Press sticks sour pins of satire into these balloon like promises. People are back from the Riviera in hordes. Or up from Italy. Or over from England. There is opera, the Russian ballet, racing, balls; it is spring and Paris is itself again. Newspaper readers write feverishly to ask who has seen the first white-breasted nut-hatch. The Paris-New York telephone rings seventy times in one day. The Montparnasse poets, if there are any left among the crowds of tourists who push about the Dome and the Rotonde in search of Bohemia, confirm the fact that spring is here.

The Bois has suddenly come to life like a salamander. The smart restaurants do not open officially for several weeks. But on fine days they are crowded at tea or luncheon. Their gardens are bright with spring flowers timed to bloom for the formal opening, but pleasant enough now. Riders dash up for an aperitif on horseback and canter off without dismounting. I saw the entire staff of one of the most correct of the Bois restaurants playing soccer across the road from its impressive portals. It was eleven-thirty of a fine spring morning. The head waiter, immaculate and starched, was managing to be very athletic without mussing his vast impeccable shirt front. The wine waiter was unbending to a degree, pursuing the ball which was being spirited away by a porter in a striped waistcoat and a kitchen boy. All very informal for a staff that usually looks impassively on royalty.

Paul Poiret, not to be outdone by Paul Reboux, has come out as editor of a cook book, a selection of his favorite recipes. This suggests several developments. Perhaps all the famous dressmakers will take up culinary sidelines, along with perfumes and jewelry. One can imagine the chic of a dinner by Chanel. Theatre programs could say the star was "dressed and fed by Jenny." A gala menu would be soup by Vionnet, roast, a good hearty red ensemble by Poiret, salad by Patou (that new green he features), and something in the way of a sweet from Lanvin.

Longchamps and Auteuil drew the smartest crowd of the season last week. Perfect weather, the Prix du President at Auteuil and the holiday re-opening of Longchamp brought out all the devotees of sport and fashion. Both courses were at their best. Adolphe Menjou, with his fiancée, faced a battery of cameras; she was photogenetically dressed in gray georgette and fur. M. Menjou is esteemed here for changing the type of moustachioed French gentleman from the unscrupulous villain of the film to a sophisti-cated and charming hero. Among the new fashion notes at the races were the usual eccentricities such as hair dyed green to match the costume, and the appearance of wooden hats. Wooden hats are not as insane as they sound, being light and polished pieces of wood, pieced together and fitted on a cloth frame, making an inlaid lacquer effect. They take a long time to make and much skilful workmanship and therefore will remain only a curious novelty. Print dresses were numerous. Scarves, which are so popu-lar this year, give a vivid note to otherwise one-tone costumes. Designs on them are often series of triangles or polka dots in the brightest of color combinations. The hats seen at the races are small and slip on almost as tightly as bathing caps. Many look like wigs, light and close-fitting. They are made often of small curled feathers, of narrow loops of velvet ribbon, of fine crocheted braid or of tiny lacquered flowers. Fox scarves are still worn, but in long throws—two or three skins instead of one shoulder piece. These are graceful and new. The light beige and honey shades are popular in cloth and fur ensembles. A new color increasingly in evidence is a bluish shade, called variously hyacinth or periwinkle.

December 15, 1928

A journalist said not long ago, deprecating a dearth of news, that *"les beaux crimes et les gentils scandals attendant en general l'époque du Salon d'Automne. Pure coincidence, bien entendu."* I don't know whether the said major crimes and minor scandals are up to the usual standard. But I am sure that a few of them may be found assembled on the walls of the salon itself. Pure coincidence, *bien entendu.* Perhaps in 2,800 exhibits, there must inevitably be a number of crimes and scandals. This, by the way, is the twenty-fifth birthday of the Salon d'Automne, and for an *enfant de Bohême* that is almost a mature age. To celebrate the anniversary there is a retrospective exhibit of famous work of past exhibitions—three rooms full of former notable exhibitors. This group, selected over a period of years, puts this season's work in the shade, but the comparison is not quite fair. The retrospect includes work by Cézanne, Renoir, Carriere, Gauguin, and Rodin among the artists who have died, and Besnard, Desvallieres, Segonzac, and Matisse among the living. The statue of "Balzac," by Rodin, dominates the stairway at this end. In the main exhibit, there are forty-two American artists showing this year. One curious general note on the salon is the lack of figure and portrait paintings. Among the rare portraits is one of "Yvonne Printemps," by Helen Marre. The high point of the sculpture was perhaps the "Venue," by Aristide Maillol, a serene Aphrodite, playing with a long necklace which is draped about her neck and clasped in her hand.

The late fall days brought about the fall of a number of other things beside the temperature. The Poincaré ministry, supposedly inviolate against the best laid plans of mice and men, took a temporary tumble. Unlike Humpty Dumpty, it seems to be about to put itself together again rather neatly. Other collapses, architectural this time instead of governmental, include an epidemic of buildings falling down. Vincennes had the first ominous one. Then one night just about nine o'clock, as a heavy camion rolled by, a terrific crash was heard just off the Champs-Elysées. It proved to be the incompleted building at the corner of the rue Quentin Bauchart, on the site of what was once the mansion of the Duke de Gramont. Included in the crash was a theatre which was to have opened in April as the "Theatre Nouveau." And included in the crowd who rushed up, pale and excited to see what had happened, was M. Louis Verneuil, who had an option on the theatre. Fortunately, due to the hour of the accident, there were no people injured; but a number of cement pillars will have to be set up again. Perhaps the restless and choleric shade of the late Duke may not be satisfied with the transformation of his property. As he is described in his daughter's memoirs he would be capable of upheavals even of cement that irritated him. The recent collapses bring up a serious question for Paris. So many of the old buildings reverberate with each passing autobus, and shake with the increasing agitation of the traffic. Camions are merciless to the nerves of fine old buildings that were built for a gentler, less mechanical age. And people who sit and listen to their Sèvres tea cups rattling in the cupboard to the rhythm of passing motor trucks and busses wonder if they were not wiser to leave their ancestral apartments and move to the country.

June 1, 1929

That noble animal, the horse, is sportively and socially in the public eye this week. The Inch family, heroes of Philip Barry's late play, "White Wings," would find Paris a paradise at the moment, so given is it to equine glorification. The Concours Hippique is drawing crowds to the Grand Palais. And racing at Longchamp is about to reopen.

It is ironic to see the numbers of large shining motors waiting the horse enthusiasts outside the Grand Palais. Everyone goes to the horse show here; it is a Parisian event. People who remember the Boulevards in 1900 with their sleek, high-stepping horses, weep for the return of the motorless carriage. There are discussions in the newspapers of the good old horsey days, time of traditions and elegance. There are also younger-generation discussions of whether ladies should ride astride (not yet permitted in the horse show here) or side-saddle. Many conversations begun last year at the horse show are finished at this one, and so on, from one year to the next.

There is an excellent revue at the Marigny Theater. It is one of the most amusing ones I have seen, fresh and crisp as a spring salad. M. Saint Granier, who acts in it, is co-author with M. Le Seyeux. It revives in one part the 1900 period, an evocation that is greeted by gales of laughter, reminiscent chuckles from the older part of the audience and incredulous giggles from the younger members. A day in the life of a belle at the time of the Paris exposition is the theme. Jane Marnac rises from her couch long haired and ruffled, dons countless starched petticoats and high buttoned boots and goes forth to a gay life of twenty-eight years ago. Dinner at a smart café (chicken six francs, wine four! they are robbing you!) brought tears to the eyes of the audience. A scene from a revue at the Marigny of the period brings back languorous waltzes, some absurd songs sung by Dramen from the beginning of his career, and several frankly antiquated jokes. A charming period it is for revue purposes, not too far away to have historical dignity, but near enough for the hats and the gestures to be ridiculous. I hope this comes to New York, whole or adapted.

The curator of the Carnavalet museum, in a more solemn effort, is having an exposition of life in the Eighteenth Century—every-day life in Paris, carefully reconstructed from furniture and in two parts, middle ages to 1880 in the rue de Rivoli side of the Louvre; from 1880 to to-day in the Musée du Jeu de Paume. The exhibit was opened by Prince Eugene, youngest brother of the King of Sweden. Prince Eugene is himself a distinguished painter and several of his vivid landscapes hang in the exhibit.

Decidedly the popular heroine of the moment is Jeanne d'Arc. There are pageants and parades and superfilms in her memory. Every young equestrian hopes at least once to be chosen to play Joan. One of the most carefully organized events was the pageant that ended the Horse Show. Mlle. De Molitor, the eighteen-year-old daughter of the Baronne Molitor, took the part of Jeanne. Tall, slim, and blonde, she is known as the best equestrian in France—no mean title that. She rode lately in the Pau hunt and says much of her skill came from that and from the excellent *maître d'equipages* who coached her. She has also hunted boar, a sport that demands skill and endurance. In the pageant she was surrounded by the 12th cuirassiers, in the uniforms of the period. The standard bearer was young de la Tremoille, a descendant of the historic de la Tremoille, taking the part of his ancestor in the pageant. All the details of armor, costumes, and lances were done with historical accuracy. No more effective Joan will ride than this one.

"What College Did to Me,"
College Humor, *1926*

"What College did to me?"

Imagine asking anyone who graduated in '18 or '19 such a question! According to the young sprouts of the class of '29, who are the present life of the educational party, the following scene ensues. . . .

Mrs. Benét, her lace cap over her sparse gray hair and putting on two pairs of strong spectacles, begins her memoirs in a faint, trembling Spencerian hand. "What," she calls feebly to that good old man, her husband, perhaps a little prematurely deaf and rheumaticky, "happened in '18, Stephen?" (They had Biblical names in those days.)

"Well, let's see, I forget," says he, ruminating quaintly through his beard. "Well, there was a war for one thing."

"What war?" says '29. "Was he with the Confederates?"

I have not forgotten the dinner we went to a year or so ago, a celebration for a young writer, class of '24, who had just finished a brilliant first play and had immediately achieved fame, marriage, movie rights and all the present gifts of the gods, and was literally eating his cake and having it too. We started out, a sprightly cheerful pair. Gathered there were dozens of stalwart Princeton '23s and blooming Wellesley '24's. There was a respectful hush as we came into the room. I suddenly realized we were the chaperones! We left feeling a not very well preserved one hundred and eighty, poor and decrepit—and they were probably glad we left early. The place for the old is bed.

I remember hearing in a musical comedy, years ago, that the first signs of old age are (1) when you prefer baked apples to raw ones and (2) when all the policemen begin to look younger and younger to you. Well, I can still eat raw apples (I still have my teeth, though according to the ads, four out of five do not) but the undergraduates certainly look younger every year to me. Some come straight to college from kindergarten.

Every now and then at reunions, undergraduates—mere children—come up to Steve and say respectfully in a brave, manly, way, "How are you, *sir?*" And their sisters make little ducks at me.

I remember with wrath the charming young lady from Bryn Mawr (blonde bob, and a general idea of finishing in 1930) who said to me sweetly across the table at dinner, getting courage with the salad course,

"And has your little son started school yet, Mrs. Benét, and will you plan to send him to Yale?"

"My daughter," I remarked coldly, "is not yet ten months old, and while she *is* precocious, I have not yet thought of school."

"Well, send her to Yale," whispered the man at my left. He was Harvard, I think. "By the time she's old enough it will probably be co-ed. And cheer up, when your daughter does go to college, that little idiot will have wrinkles and a transformation."

"And I suppose I'll have one foot in the grave by then," said I, hoping to be contradicted.

"Try glands," he suggested consolingly. "They're the hope of the aged."

At least I have been spared the shock of a young officer out of West Point ten years, who had been too busy since in Germany and its environs, to notice encroaching middle age.

"What!" said a sprightly flapper at his last reunion. "Up to see your son graduate?"

I admit that it gives me a creepy feeling to find the class of 1930 hard upon us. *Thirty* sounds so odd, somehow. And I find myself, when people ask me my class—why do people ask your exact class so often?—saying airily, "Oh, before twenty."

It is not only a difference in time. The customs of the country have changed and the language. We must have lived in a sort of mid-Victorian calm. Think of fur coats and flopping socks and galoshes, the Charleston and cross-word puzzles, at least in such flocks, being rare birds. Lines were snappy, but not the ultra-modern kind that bark and bite. The more I read the latest, last, positively youngest generation college novels, the more I realize what sheltered and cloistered lives ours were, and *how we really don't know anything about life.*

Someone (I suggest COLLEGE HUMOR), ought to do a Family Album of College Life. Begin back in the 1860's when a cautious and prosperous beer magnate founded one of our best known women's colleges, then called a "Female Seminary," with the bold and forward looking sentiment that ladies could *perhaps* (see Godey's *Lady's Book,* 1862) "instruct the young and become missionaries," the same era when boys at Harvard and Yale came to college with hounds and a hunter (and earlier, slaves). Through the period when Aunt Theodosia in puffed sleeves and stays, and Uncle Roderick with long curling mustachios and antiquated sweater first enjoyed the benefits of co-education . . . down, down, or up, up, depending on your present viewpoint, to the glittering present of bobs and the sports model.

Have you ever looked in the old year books of 1890? The dashing, languishing Don Juans who made up the football teams and the glee clubs looked forty at least, even in their freshman year. Have you tried to understand the jests about tallyhos and pompadours and decided they were all rather silly—and wondered why on earth they took such odd, dull subjects as Greek and Latin when they could better develop themselves for a Bigger and Better Future by studying Ornithology or Practical Pelmanism? Well, list them and put them alongside our present peccadillos. Nineteen eighteen is old stuff now—but so will 1928 be in time, said she morosely. The Charleston will be a quaint old folk dance eventually, and jokes about Oxford bags and sliding socks quite incomprehensible without a glossary.

Autres temps, autres mœurs; yes, yes, I went to school in France for a year.

Why doesn't someone write novels about colleges west of Albany, anyway? The Middle West, with a few exceptions, is as untouched literarily, as when La Salle and De Soto found it.

Unfortunately for me, I went to a middle western university and now live in the East. Or perhaps I should say, I went to a middle western university and now live in the East, unfortunately. I once met a provincial gentleman from Yale whose western boundary was Buffalo.

"Where did you go to college?" said he.

"At the University of Chicago," said I.

"What?" said, he, as though I had said I had spent four years gathering camels in the Libyan desert.

"Yes," said I helpfully, trying out the principles of a public speaking course about talking to an audience in terms it can understand. "You know, President Angell—you've heard of him—well, he was there for years."

"*What?*" said he. And went right out to look at President Angell again.

I graduated from one of the best universities in the country. There I am being modest. If you asked me right out, I should say the best university in the country. It has an excellent faculty, library, standard, endowment— everything that makes a university what it should be. I am tired of meeting people in New York who say, "Where?" at me. There are too many people whose collegiate map groups the University of Chicago, Michigan and Leland Stanford hazily in middle Colorado, allowing a large open reserve in Idaho for a flock of state universities. If someone would only write a Baedeker and get up a Cook's tour of them, what a splendid horizon would open.

What I meant to say at the beginning of this article, ladies and gentlemen, was that from ten to five years ago I spent four years at the University of Chicago, and one at the Ecole Normale Superieure at Sevres outside Paris. They did a great deal for me. I am not thinking of trading them for any other five years I have heard of since.

"Pussy-Cat, Pussy-Cat Where Have You Been?"
Harper's Bazaar, *October 1930*

Returning after three years abroad, you feel like—you feel like Rip Van Winkle. You have left undone all the things that other people have done; you may or may not have done a few things that they have not done, but how to get them into the conversation! And, to continue with the church service, there is often no health in you—no conversational health, at least—or so you feel in New York's brilliant X-ray sunlight.

Backgammon, you say? Backgammon. You seem to remember having seen Backgammon boards in antique shops, or was that chess? Or perhaps you think of Uncle Lemuel who used to while away placid evenings with that ancient pastime. Backgammon, you are informed, is the latest form of indoor sport. Murder games, which had just begun to take their toll of shattered nerves in Paris, have gone out.

And you discover crooners. Singing when you left, if done at all, was gone about in a large, gusty, open-throated way. No ear-straining was required on the part of the listeners; quite the reverse. Now you are asked to admire favourites who inhale their voices as they do their cigarettes and who expel them through what seems to be a wet sponge in the mouth. There is the same warm, damp muffled effect in the vocal organs. Very pleasant and soothing when you are used to it. But so surprising the first time.

And pent-houses! Pent-houses, each with a major, magnificent view and a minor, microscopic rock garden, have sprung up in the most unimaginable places. In fact one of my first experiences on returning was to pause, bemused, in the midst of traffic at the sight of what had happened to Fifty-seventh Street since I had left it. "Well, Pocahontas," remarked the traffic cop, "watcha looking at?" Then I knew I was back.

People live in new places. There are few constants left. Your address book must be erased and scratched beyond recognition. You learn futuristic telephone exchanges such as Volunteer and Bogardus. People have migrated to the East River. They have climbed up and up in new buildings. You shoot heavenward in incredibly swift elevators to find them. Were elevators ever so breathtaking five years ago? More incredibly still, after the one-way-up-only Paris *ascenseurs*, you shoot down again.

Even foods are different. You are initiated to the tomato juice cocktail, for instance, which now graces every menu card and which I never remember seeing in the old days. Gustatory surprises before dinner include an Arabian Nights profusion of little sandwiches wrapped in bacon. One friend, always up on the latest dietetic fads, cordially suggested that I try a raw liver sandwich. I declined with horror, only to have her tell me that this is the modern diet for healthy children. And water, of course, flows like wine in Paris.

Diseases are transformed. Glands and sinuses are in. Old-fashioned liverishness (which is still a favourite complaint in England) and the deadly *courant d'air* which is the basis of all ailments in France, do not exist here. A happy change, on the whole. I much prefer to hear about the vagaries of the thyroid to the liver, if the conversation must get medical.

Even antiques, which ought to be reasonably constant since they mirror another static age, have changed. Model stage-coaches replace ships in bottles. Crystal lustres have been mysteriously found and resurrected in quantity. Old dolls, bright painted toys, porcelain dogs and the like have migrated from the back shelves in the nursery to the very front of the antique store windows.

You have read none of the latest, hot-from-the-press best sellers. Nor seen the last plays. There are six-months conversational cycles. Try to vary them too much and you sound stupid or erudite; either of which makes for the same conversational aridity.

There is no end to the list of what you have forgotten: the length of little boys' trousers; the number of coloured people; the popularity of a certain bleak form of Early American decorating; the cleanliness, the super-cleanliness; the enormous ice-boxes, the sun coming up in waves from the pavement; the cathedral-like drug stores where you can buy a four-course luncheon, a Kodak, some hardware and the complete works of Mr. Conrad; the small door-keys, after your four-inch iron Paris one; the extremes of hot and cold water, the politeness (in porters and moving men but not in plumbers); the number seven written without a cross-bar; the splendid offices, looking for all the world like huge, bright kindergartens. All these strike you afresh, as if you had just seen them for the first time, with particular clearness, like the sudden clarity after coming out of an anesthetic.

The problem is not the much-heralded how to speak French to the waiter, but how not to speak French to the waiter and be laughed at. There is nothing so ridiculous as dragging a foreign language by its heels just to show it off. The people who just cannot speak their mother tongue without interlarding, *Voilà tout, Ma Chère, Dios Mio,* and things like that, we have all disliked always; to be taken for one of these irritating show-offs is too shameful to think of. And yet I defy anyone who has shouted *"Entrez"* over a considerable period of time when someone taps at the door, to change suddenly to crying "Come in" without considerable mental effort. Habit grips you. You say good morning and good-by automatically on entering and leaving a shop, and are stared at uneasily. You speak of mounting and descending the stairway, keeping French locutions, and sound incredibly affected. You are uncertain about the price of a newspaper, car-fare, tipping. "Well," people say, "How silly!" and return the verdict "spoiled" instead of ever the kindlier "absent-minded." You watch your children carefully through the phases of a musical comedy accent, hoping and praying that theirs will not be the sad fate of the bilingual little boy who, in an unguarded moment, called his shirt his chemise and was not allowed to forget it through the rest of his school career.

This constant effort to bridge over lapses, to catch up, to find out what people are talking and thinking! It is exactly like Alice's breathless run with the Red Queen; on and on furiously you go, to arrive triumphantly, panting, contemporaneous, just where you should have started. I know of no feeling like it. Except skipping classes in school in the old days. To be put with older, taller, wiser children who have had fractions and irregular verbs in French. And to try to proceed smilingly and not too stupidly with lessons that preclude a knowledge of these same fractions and verbs. Substitute conversation, small talk, fads, interests of the moment—and you have it. A good deal of home work is necessary.

Things change so quickly in this fluid modern life. Pussy-cat, Pussy-cat, where have you been?

"Twinkle, Twinkle, Little Star,"
Vogue, *February 1, 1931*

SCENE—a crowded waiting-room. Appointments have been made a long, long time before. There is not an empty chair in the place. Eight women are waiting somewhat uneasily; women of all kinds and types—old and young—shabby and smart, one so well known to the rotogravure sections that she is bending behind a large magazine, vainly hoping to be unnoticed. Like an ostrich with its head in the sand. Two prosperous business men rush in and out hastily for brief consultations. Every one has the absent-minded, introspective look of the person who has a long story to unfold.

Where are we? Visiting a doctor? A psychoanalyst? A lawyer? Not at all. An astrologer.

Are you unhappy in love? Consult an astrologer. Did you lose in the stock market? Ditto. Do you suffer from sinus, arthritis, or any of the fashionable gland diseases? Ditto. In some extreme cases, astrology becomes a religion in itself. Twinkle, twinkle, little star, how I (and everybody else, at the present moment) wonder what you are!

The astrologers' scope is limitless, as wide as the heavens; love, business, health all being subjects affected by the stars. They tell you in what latitude you can live happily. (This often inconveniently turns out to be Port Said or Northern and Western Africa.) They advise careers. (Mine says I would do well and meet with success "in any business connected with liquids and shipping"; can that be bootlegging?) They tell you when it is best to marry or to stay single. These marriages are literally made in heaven.

My introduction to astrology was typical. We had been invited to dinner in Paris by some people we didn't know very well. A few days before the dinner, my hostess telephoned me.

"Would you mind telling me your birthday, dear?"

"My birthday?" I repeated, wondering if I had heard aright, or if this were again the fault of the French telephone.

"Yes, your birthday. You see, I'm arranging my dinner-table, and it will help me so much. Just a minute while I get a pencil and paper."

"She says she wants to know my birthday so she can arrange her dinner-table," I said to my listening husband.

"Sounds like Alice in Wonderland to me," said he. "Are you sure she said *Birthday?*"

"My BIRTHday?" I shouted into the telephone. "Well, it's January fourteenth."

"Tell her you like silk stockings usually," came from my side.

"Oh, that's fine," she said approvingly. I felt relieved that I had not done too badly.

"And your husband?"

"His is July twenty-second."

"Oh, born on the cusp."

"No, in Bethlehem, Pennsylvania."

"I meant on the turn between Cancer and Leo. Well, thank you so much. You see, this is a group of people who don't know one another well, and I did want to have congenial people next each other. Now it's all going to work out beautifully."

And that dinner *was* ruled over by celestial harmony. Every one got on. No one asked Mr. X, who is known as the White Father of the Paris Colony, how long he had been in Paris, or the French diplomat if he spoke French. People who talked nothing but golf and polo did not have to chat with spoilsports who didn't know one stick from the other. It was miraculous. I said so to the gentleman on my right, who proved to be a scoffer. "Miraculous! It's just confidence. Faith! She's sure things'll go well, so they do. There is nothing worse than one of those nervous hostesses. She stares at you worriedly if the shadow of a silence comes near your place at the table, and that either paralyses you or makes you break out into a bright red rash of small talk. Of course, she'd say we got on because of the friendly aspect of your Jupiter, or something like that."

She would also, I reflected, have some excellent celestial reason for his being such a sceptic. "Poor Peter, how can he help but be material-minded with his threatening Uranus!"

"When is your birthday?" is no longer an idle question, but one that may disclose your past, present, and future. Children's birthdays are planned for propitious dates—as nearly as this can be done with whimsical Mother Nature upsetting calculations. Plans are made to give you a phlegmatic child or a temperamental will-o'-the-wisp. The choice is yours. Some mothers insist on a stop-watch as part of the maternity equipment of the modern hospital to mark the exact moment of birth. The exact moment of birth, by the way, astrologically speaking, is the first cry. "Then the child calls out and makes itself known to the universe, and the universe rushes in upon it." For better, for worse!

Children's horoscopes are plotted with great solemnity the instant they arrive. It is undeniably convenient to know that you have a potential Napoleon or Helen of Troy to raise, or even to tell the difference between the common or garden varieties in infants—the horny-thorny-Capricorny child from a bounding son of Leo. If mothers are more than a little inclined to find remarkable things in their children's horoscopes—just the genius strain—don't blame either astrology or the astrologer. The human element is fatally apt to disarrange any science and is the basis of most of the good stories about this one. We all remember delightedly that our horoscope said we had unusual intelligence and intuition and forget that it also spoke of selfishness and peculiarities of temperament. A good astrologer is as impersonal and discreet as a physician. "You are the only person in the world who knows my real age," said one lady I know to her astrologer, "and if it ever gets out I'll know who told!" Such dire tendencies as kleptomania and other skeletons in the closet are supposed to be shown in the horoscope. Suppose, perish the thought, the astrologer gossiped.

The extremes to which the cult has been carried are no reflection on astrology itself and make some of its best stories. I heard of a woman who bought an expensive dog in a shop because its birth date coincided with her own. (Could it be that the wily pet-shop keeper had heard of astrology?) "Oh, yes, Madame, I would advise the Great Dane rather than the Pekingese. He is a genuine Gemini. And the Sealyham, while its pedigree is not so fine, was born during an eclipse and ought to prove very unusual."

Another fan said to me, "Oh, I didn't even look for a house for the summer. What was the use? I wouldn't have found anything until next month anyhow, and all that time wasted!" In the midst of the swirling taxis in the place de la Concorde, I had a friend shout in my ear, "Look out. I must be careful. I'm in the worst accident phase of the year." Another devotee goes to bed on unlucky days fraught with evil omen and stays there, where presumably, unless Saturn makes the ceiling of the room fall on her, she will be safe.

You can even have the horoscope of an idea cast. In case you have an inspiration for a play, get out your watch and mark down the minute the thought came to you, and you'll know whether your name will be up in lights on Broadway. Perhaps. Or cast the horoscope of the Republican party and Yale college and win all your election and football bets. Some do.

"I have found that clothes bought with the moon in Scorpio never last; they either wear out too soon or get torn or burned quickly." Fancy finding you had bought your new Chanel with the Moon in Scorpio! And imagine how this may react on the clothing business. Let us hope that it will be compensated for by another cult that works out congenial symbols in colour vibrations and says if you have sinus you must be surrounded by yellow, or if arthritis, you must live in green. Which is all very fine for the curtain dealers. The modern decorators, by the way, have been doing a thriving business with horoscopic motifs. I saw a lovely star and moon perched on top of a penthouse. Maps of the heavens make good murals. There are even horoscopic perfumes.

Big and Little Troubles

Next to love problems, which drive the greatest number to consult the occult, people seek explanations for their troubles from astrologers. Large business depressions and small annoyances need to be rationalized. I remember, once, mourning because my Siamese cat had died. "Plenty of your pet cats will die in the next months" prophesied my astrologer friend, "Saturn is in Capricorn." She proved only too right. Saturn is the celestial schoolmaster, a rigid taskmaster who gives you a few hard whacks in the way of lessons and some sparse but doubly sweet rewards after, if you live through the lessons. Not so much battle, murder, and sudden death. Just minor catastrophes such as breaking your best Spode teacups, catching the flu, leaks in the bathtub, and missing wills. In case Saturn is not bothering you, your troubles may be due to Mars or Uranus. There is surely an astrologic explanation. While Saturn was in Capricorn, I lost my new necklace and sat into green paint with my favourite Paris dress, and the children got whooping cough, and the steel bonds shrank, and the drain pipes leaked, and the maid left the window open so that rain blew in torrents on the brocade of my favourite chair. Oh yes, and the Sealyhams puppies turned out not to be sired by Highborn Harry after all, but by the unworthy gentleman of Mrs. Sealyham's choice, a mangy Pomeranian next door. And I bored everyone by talking about my troubles. A complete washout of a winter, all because of Saturn sending down saturnine beams.

The extreme present excitement in astrology and the occult generally has excellent historical precedent. Always we have had pseudo-scientific fads that have enjoyed great popularity. Like the poor, they are always with us. Marie Antoinette and her court ladies literally fell under the spell of Mesmer. Frederick Anthony Mesmer, an eighteenth-century physician, had evolved a theory of animal magnetism hypnotism, finally called after him, mesmerism. Banished from the court of Empress Marie Theresa, he found a patron in her daughter and her attendants who sat spellbound about an iron tank, expecting a mysterious galvanic fluid would wash away their troubles.

It was phrenology and fortune telling in the 'sixties and 'seventies. Victorian ladies who had married silky-mustachioed villains discovered that their mutual incompatibility of temper was all due to the fact that his bump of combativeness—scarcely perceptible under the thick curling wig—was excessive. Gentle maidens of the 'sixties went apprehensively to phrenologists. Their meek heads were thumped and bumped and whacked, and the verdict was always slightly disappointing. That protuberance you got from falling from your perambulator in childhood? Very well. Beware of a coarse brunette gentleman with a hasty temper who will bring you much unhappiness. That majestic forehead inherited from your maternal grandfather, hitherto a matter for pride, might or might not mean something dire. Phrenology was undoubtedly responsible for the elaborate hair arrangements of the period. Long curls and thick bangs, bushy masculine sideburns, and lovelocks could hide some of the fatal evidence, mounts of avariciousness, humps of temper, and the like. It is less easy to conceal a dull horoscope from the omniscient astrologer.

And fortune tellers! Godey's Ladies Book has dozens of stories in which the crux of the plot is where the fair heroine is warned that she will be unhappy in love unless she finds a hero with Scotch ancestors and a mole on his left cheek. Apparently, there was a fortune teller under every Victorian bush. The heroine always went on her secret errand of peering into the future swathed heavily in veils—unlike the present star-gazers who start out boldly, taking all their friends with them, if possible.

Figures Don't Lie

Numerology, that second cousin of astrology, has many followers. It involves a brisk drill in simple arithmetic. Mathematical harmony is its basic principle. Add up your birth date, day, month, and year. Add up your name, the letters of the alphabet being represented by a scale one to nine. The result must be in harmony, or you'll never succeed. You invariably discover your name is wrong. Instead of Jane and John, you find you should be called Pyramus and Thisbe. Several authentic celebrities are cited as evidence that change in name brought fame and fortune. But how to get one's friends and family to remember to call one Amaryllis instead of Lucy, even in the hope of a career? The large banks have lately complained at the number of accounts that have had name changes. Mary Jones to Wandine Jones and the like, showing the present wide-spread belief in numerology.

Too fervent faith in these earlier fads was frowned on by the devoutly religious. They feared them as superstitions, work of the Evil One. The Victorian lady, for that reason, did not dare trespass far in the fields of the occult. This fear has vanished for her modern sister who thinks nothing of trying crystal-gazing, having her handwriting read, and going in for astrology all in the same season.

There are many theories as to the WHY of the fast growing popularity of our new—or rather, ancient—cult. It has become a science, not a superstition, say its devotees. It explains life, is constructive in an age that is notably chaotic. All Nature, we are told, runs in mathematical cycles, stars, moon, tides, days, and months. The key lies in astrology and numerology. At any rate, you can use up a great many pieces of paper working it out.

Words of Warning

If you are going to follow this trend and take up astrology, do go to a reputable, experienced astrologer; (and make an appointment a long time ahead). For making a horoscope, whether you believe in it or not, is a considerable job, involving time, skill, study, and intuition. Serious work as done by a competent astrologer can not be compared with the amateur calculations of ladies who stick pins in a map of the heavens under the impression that they are figuring something out. The latter may be a form of amusement, but it has nothing to do with any known science. It may be art, but it is certainly not astrology—any more than building houses out of blocks is architecture. A great deal of study is involved in making out even a simple accurate chart, and more text books than the amateur can ever possibly get together. You must look up the latitude and longitude of your birthplace, find out the exact moment of birth if possible—a thing our less occult-minded mothers often carelessly failed to jot down. Great discrepancies may come in if you forget about daylight-saving time, for instance. The actual heavens furnish new discoveries that mean more charting. If numerology involves a brisk drill in arithmetic, astrology lures you into mathematics, geography, astronomy, and further afield.

Astrologists prophesied the last war. As to future prophecy, they seem fixed about the date of the next world cataclysm. Although they differ on other points, they agree that 1942 is the date for the next catastrophe, either war, earthquake, or revolution. They think that it may be in the East and not affect America as profoundly as other countries.

One question every one puts to them, according to astrologers—Wouldn't two persons born at the same time at the same place have exactly the same horoscope? The answer is Yes. There is one famous example of a man born the same hour, the same day, and in the same place as the Kaiser. It was discovered that he married at the same moment, had the same number of children, approximately the same diseases, and that when the Kaiser inherited the throne this man inherited his father's little business. It was brought to the Kaiser's attention, and he endowed his astrological twin. Just lately, there was an interesting case: twins who had an accident on different roads—one fell from a horse, the other hit by a motor-truck; both were brought to the hospital in the interval of half an hour. The parents who had rushed to see one met the other coming in as they were leaving. Differences in the case of real twins are accounted for by the interval of time between the two births, which often brings heavenly changes. Also, in later life, the horoscope of wife or husband modifies the partner's.

There is a story of one of the most famous astrologers in America. The law still regards any kind of fortune-telling, or peering into the future, as a variant of the shell game and hailed this lady into court to prove to the magistrate why she shouldn't be arrested as a faker. Whereupon she asked the judge his son's birthday and gave his horoscope so accurately, intelligently, and neatly that she was released, having proved to that arm of the law at least that she was a scientist and not a faker.

More than any other means of divination, astrology is taken seriously. The discussion about it has made two armed camps, the converts and the scoffers. The army of the converts is increasing. Will astrology continue its present vogue, waxing more and more popular, until we learn to work out our own charts, as the devotees claim? Or will it be supplanted by another belief?

Well, all wisdom is written in the stars, say the astrologers.

Selected Bibliography

Arlen, Michael. *The Green Hat*. New York: Doran, 1923.

Bacon, Leonard. *Semi-centennial*. New York: Harper, 1939.

Benét, Laura. *When William Rose, Stephen Vincent and I Were Young*. New York: Dodd, Mead, 1976.

Benét, Stephen Vincent, *Selected Letters of Stephen Vincent Benét*. Edited by Charles Fenton. New Haven, Conn.: Yale University Press, 1960.

Benét, William Rose. *The Dust Which Is God*. New York: Dodd, Mead, 1941.

Cabell, James Branch. *Some of Us: An Essay in Epitaphs*. New York: Robert M. McBride, 1930.

Colum, Mary. "In Memory of Elinor Wylie." *New Republic*, Feb. 6, 1929, 317–19.

Farr, Judith. *The Life and Art of Elinor Wylie*. Baton Rouge: Louisiana State University Press, 1983.

Fenton, Charles. *Stephen Vincent Benét: The Life and Times of an American Man of Letters, 1898-1943*. New Haven, Conn.: Yale University Press, 1958.

Fitzgerald, F. Scott. *Letters of F. Scott Fitzgerald*. Edited by Andrew Turnbull. New York: Charles Scribner's Sons, 1953.

———. *A Life in Letters*. Edited by Matthew Bruccoli. New York: Charles Scribner's Sons, 1994.

Gould, Jean. *The Poet and Her Book: A Biography of Edna St. Vincent Millay*. New York: Dodd, Mead, 1969.

Hively, Evelyn Helmick. *A Private Madness: The Genius of Elinor Wylie*. Kent, Ohio: Kent State University Press, 2003.

Izzo, David Garrett, and Lincoln Konkle, eds. *Stephen Vincent Benét: Essays on His Life and Work*. Jefferson, N.C.: McFarland, 2003.

Kuhl, Nancy. *Intimate Circles: American Women in the Arts.* New Haven, Conn.: Beinecke Rare Book and Manuscript Library, Yale University, 2003.

McAndrew, Patricia. "Stephen and Rosemary: A Love Story." In *Stephen Vincent Benét: Essays on His Life and Work,* edited by David Garrett Izzo and Lincoln Konkle, 37–71. Jefferson, N.C.: McFarland, 2003.

Norris, Kathleen. *Butterfly.* New York: A. L. Burt, 1923.

———. *Family Gathering.* Garden City, N.Y.: Doubleday, 1959.

Olson, Stanley. *Elinor Wylie: A Life Apart.* New York: Dial, 1979.

Potter, Nancy A. J. *Elinor Wylie: A Biographical and Critical Study.* PhD diss., Boston University, 1954.

Ridge, Lola. "For E.W." *Saturday Review of Literature,* July 20, 1929, 1187.

Ryan, Charles A. Riley II. *The Jazz Age in France.* New York: Harry N. Abrams, 2004.

Stroud, Perry. *Stephen Vincent Benét.* New York: Twayne, 1962.

Tomkins, Calvin. *Living Well Is the Best Revenge.* New York: New American Library, 1972.

Vaill, Amanda. *Everybody Was So Young.* New York: Broadway Books, 1999.

Van Doren, Charles. "Elinor Wylie: A Portrait from Memory." *Harper's,* Sept. 1936, 358–67.

Van Hoosen, Bertha. *Petticoat Surgeon.* Chicago: Peoples Book Club, 1947.

Wilson, Edmund. *The Twenties.* Introduction by Leon Edel. New York: Farrar, Straus and Giroux, 1975.

Wylie, Elinor. *Selected Works of Elinor Wylie.* Edited by Evelyn Helmick Hively. Kent, Ohio: Kent State University Press, 2005.

Index